FIRST PERSON, SINGULAR

First Person, Singular

Genevieve Caldwell

THOMAS NELSON PUBLISHERS
Nashville • Camden • New York

Published in Nashville, Tennessee, by Thomas Nelson, Inc. and distributed in Canada by Lawson Falle, Ltd., Cambridge, Ontario.

Printed in the United States of America.

Unless otherwise noted the Scripture version used in this publication is THE NEW KING JAMES VERSION. Copyright © 1979, 1980, 1982, Thomas Nelson, Inc., Publishers.

Library of Congress Cataloging-in-Publication Data

Caldwell, Genevieve.
    First person singular.

    1. Single women.   2. Single women—United States.
3. Single women—Religious life.   I. Title.
HQ800.2.C35   1986   305.4'890652   86-18115
ISBN 0-8407-3072-1

In memory of
Mom and Dad

CONTENTS

I don't even write letters, so I certainly never expected to write a book. God delights in the unexpected. It gives him the opportunity to use not just one person, but many to bring about his purposes.

Of the many people who helped bring this book about, first on my list to thank is Dr. Larry Crabb, Professor of Psychology at Grace Theological Seminary. Originally my counselor and then my mentor, he gave me tough feedback on the subject of a single woman's sexuality as well as her attitude toward work. Not only did he allow me to use his Model for Biblical Counseling in Chapter 11, he also did what he does so well—he encouraged me greatly. Thanks.

Second, my appreciation goes to Carol Weissenborn who has made this book substantially more readable than it would have been without her. Her editing and poking holes in my arguments tightened my writing as well as my thoughts.

Third, there would be no book without single women themselves. So, in addition to Carol, I thank Janet and Joyce Sisler who believed from the beginning that what I was writing should be published, Sue Manton for her midnight hours at the word processor, Melody and my prayer group for their emotional and prayer support, and the many single women who shared their lives with me.

God has been good in bringing about the unexpected. I am grateful to him.

I am something of a cynic. When one has been a pastor as long as I have, one begins to realize that not everything that portrays itself as "Christian" really is Christian and not everything that is advertised as "helpful" really is helpful.

A couple of years ago I read a book that moved me very deeply, but my cynicism, always the "quiet monster" in the back of my mind, created all sorts of questions about the book: Does this man really live what he writes? How honest is he with his words? Is he writing what he *hopes* is true or what he *knows* is true? I was speaking at a college near this author's home and I expressed my doubts to a friend of mine who was also a friend of the author. He said, "Steve, believe me, he illustrates every word of his book!" As soon as I got home I reread the book, taking the time to underline and absorb the words that had come from an "honest pen."

As a friend and pastor to Genevieve Caldwell, I want to do for you what my friend did for me. I want to tell you the truth about her. Gigi Caldwell is an illustration of her book. She knows the experience of applying biblical truth to your life. Here is a woman who has struggled with the real issues of singleness—facing the tensions, dealing with the hard questions, and, above all, testing biblical Christianity by confirming its truth in her life. And we are the beneficiaries.

If you are single, this book will make you feel good about yourself. You will find here the kind of honesty and compassion one hopes to find, but seldom does, in books from Christian singles. If you are married, don't think this book is just for "them." Many of the issues you face are not that different from those that are faced by singles. You will find here a new appreciation for singles and a new sensitivity to their needs. And men, don't think Gigi has nothing to say to you. Her strong words challenge our thinking about women and our relationships with them.

If you don't like honesty, then you should put this book down right now. If you would rather live in the Disney World of Christian cliches, you are not going to like this book. If you prefer to avoid the hard issues, this is not for you.

But, for the rest of you, hang on. This book came from an "honest pen."

Steve Brown, Pastor
Key Biscayne Presbyterian Church

When I became a widow at twenty-six, I thought my life was over. Desperate, almost in a daze, I took my two-year-old son and moved to Paris to live while I did postgraduate work in design. Paris was new to me then. It was exciting and incredibly beautiful. I had been accepted by a French school, my son was in a good nursery—I remember asking myself, what more could I want? I wasn't sure.

Life seemed to be interesting, even fun, but on the inside I wept. So I prayed, read my Bible, went to a Bible study, and took a lover. Took a lover! I was a Christian! Didn't I know God was supposed to be enough? Yes I did, but I wanted someone earthly to love, too.

Those were agonizing years. I had not expected my life to turn out this way. Life was supposed to be perfect—apple pie and mom, like the "Donna Reed Show."

Certainly it had started off well enough. Joe was a star quarterback for Army. I had known him since I was fourteen. We fell in love in high school in the late fifties and were married the day after we graduated from college. The wedding took place in the chapel at West Point, complete with military uniforms and crossed sabres, beautiful bridesmaids, and spring flowers. Joe was smart, strong, capable, and confident. And I was his bride. To me it seemed to be a storybook romance.

But there was more to our marriage than love and romance. I admired Joe. He trusted God. He was a godly man. And yet, a year after Joe's automobile accident, with his memory still fresh in my mind, I was in bed with another man.

Some people assume that I fell away from God during this time. I actually drew closer to God after Joe's death because I was afraid of being alone. People have asked, "But did you pray and read your Bible?" I prayed until I thought my heart would break. I spent days at a time studying God's Word, but that didn't keep me from longing for someone earthly to love.

The pattern that established itself during the three years I was in Paris became the pattern I would experience over and over again for the next twelve years. I would be feeling lonely and restless when I would meet an interesting man. The mysterious chemical attraction that exists between men and women would surface. I would sense it, be afraid, and turn to God. The man would sense my attraction to him, be interested, and then wonder what this religious thing was all about. I would struggle against my desires, but eventually we would make love. Curiously enough, the man would be a source of great comfort to me. Only after he was gone did I feel any guilt about the relationship. Then the pain would be intense.

I didn't want to sin, to turn my back on God. I just wasn't sure that God alone was enough.

When I returned to the States I became active in the church where Joe and I had grown up—in the place where I had accepted Christ at age thirteen. A Christian singles fellowship met in my house each Sunday night, and I attended a Bible study with a group of friends, most of whom were seminary students.

But didn't I feel hypocritical? Of course I did. I remember weeping, crying out, saying, "Please God, either give me a husband or give me the strength, the power to change."

My work was very important to me. After returning from Paris I threw myself into my career and opened my own business as an interior designer. It blossomed. At first there were only a few clients; then there were more. I remember the day someone told me I had become a status symbol. My work was photographed for several magazines. I did a room in the Junior League Showhouse one year and remodeled a yacht for visiting celebrities the next. Soon, I was working seventy hours a week, and there seemed to be no letup. I was exhausted.

Then, within a four-year period, I was close to bankruptcy, my mother died, my best friend died, my boyfriend died, and my son entered a difficult adolescence. My life had changed. For twelve years, things had seemed rosy. Now they were not. The reality of unavoidable pressure lent a new urgency to my faith. Once and for all I had to decide. Was God enough or not?

The pain of aloneness had always been intense, but the greatest pain of all was worrying that I had somehow messed up my son's life. More alone now than I had ever been in my entire life, I knew that neither my work nor a lover could help. What my son needed from me was an inner strength I did not have. I sought out a Christian counselor for advice.

God was gracious. He sent me to a counselor who believed in God's truth and in my ability to change. For the first time in years I had hope that I could have the strength to break my old pattern. I knew the struggle was not going to be an easy one, but my counselor encouraged me that God would be faithful.

One night, distraught and desperate, lying on my bed in a fetal position, waiting for my son to come home, worried about the direction of his life and wondering what was going to happen to him, tears began to stream down my face. I started murmuring to myself, "No one knows but you, God, no one knows but you." I repeated the phrase over and over, "No one knows but you, God, no one knows but you." Slowly but very distinctly the tone of the phrase began to change. "No one knows but you, God." I smiled. "No one knows but you." I began to laugh. "No one knows but you, God!" I laughed right out loud. God knew. And it was all okay.

God was enough!

God knew my soul, my weakness, my frame, and he was enough.

The things that had been so important to me before now faded. I had all the love I needed and was able to love in return. I was important. God had chosen me. This was the reason for my existence. It was what I had been created for.

When I think back over the years I struggled, I believe most of the time I functioned like the Israelites in Egypt. I was bound by cultural pressures and personal fears. I was one of God's people living in captivity. Yet I didn't realize this. Unconsciously, I lived with cruel taskmasters God didn't want or intend for me to have.

Taking a firm stand over any matter had never been easy for me. But with the sureness of God's love bathing my soul and with a counselor helping me analyze my thinking, I grew stronger and stronger. I gained real confidence in myself. I began to have courage. The firm, assertive, take-hold attitude needed for my son helped me in my business and my personal life as well.

One day during that time, someone asked me how I saw myself. "What do you look like in your imagination?" I had to think for a moment. I had never really noticed *me* before. I closed my eyes. I was taken aback by what I saw. I was a beautiful woman, a queen—regal, able to rule, yet feminine. I was sensitive to the king's commands.

I want to be that woman in reality. This book was written because I believe many of you do too.

PART ONE

ONE

WOMAN, MAN, & SEXUALITY

"It is not good for man to be alone. I will make a helper comparable to him." (Gen. 2:18)

SINGLE WOMEN—GOD'S UNTAPPED RESOURCE

I heard a tape on singleness the other day. The speaker said, "If you keep on believing and have faith, God will send you a husband." Nonsense. That may happen or it may not. Whether it does or not is no reflection on your faith.

For years friends said to me, "Don't worry, you'll get married again." Now they're saying, "Since you're so happy single, we're sure God is going to send you a husband." What a horrible thing to say about God—as if God waits until something doesn't matter and then offers it to us! God's not like that. He's above our manipulation.

God moves the way he chooses. What he will do about you in your singleness, I don't know. But I do know *you're not single by accident.* Your singleness makes a difference in God's world.

For five years I have thought about the issues facing Christian single women, and I believe that our singleness is part of God's overall plan to bring the light of himself into this imperfect world. In addition to struggling personally with the problems of single women, I have talked to other women for well over a thousand hours and have gone to the Father with the problems they have expressed to me. I have done this because I believe in the potential of Christian single women. I believe we are God's untapped resource. Our very aloneness is useful to him.

Yet, we sometimes don't realize this. It's difficult for us to hear the still, small voice of God when the disappointments of life are pounding in our ears.

There are two characteristics of the Christian single woman's life about which we fret. But when they're properly developed, these characteristics are assets.

The first is unencumbrance. Freedom. Our very aloneness. We are not formally bound to anyone. Our lives are literally our own.

The second is unchanneled love. We have love available to give. Because we have no mates on whom we focus that love, we can give it broadly to others.

Think of the potential in this. Women using the tender part of their natures to love others—women whose hearts have been so won by God that their sole purpose is to glorify him—can change the world.

But, you may be saying, if such love is possible, why don't we see more of it? Because we're afraid. "There they are in great fear where no fear was" (Ps. 53:5). We don't want to go for the big picture because we don't want to lose what we already have.

And because of disbelief. "Then they despised the pleasant land; they did not believe His word" (Ps.

106:24). We don't believe the promises of God and we do believe the promises of this world.

Fear and disbelief stop us. But they needn't. If we take the time to examine our fears, we will be less threatened by them. When we're less threatened, we are freer to believe God's promises.

Facing Our Needs

We all have the need for love and the need for purpose. God created each of us with the capacity for relationship with Him and for enjoying life with a purpose. When Adam and Eve rebelled against God, they shut themselves off from the best satisfaction of those needs. What God intended to be fully met capacities have become searing personal needs.

In Part I, "Woman, Man, and Sexuality," we will evaluate our need for love. Many women are influenced by their childhoods and past experiences and find it difficult to respond to men in an open and godly way. Remarks I have heard from women who are active in strong evangelical churches illustrate the broad range of emotions that Christian single women actually experience.

"I long for a man to hold me. I even long for a man to hold my hand, but no man has ever offered."

"I want desperately to be married. I can't believe God would give me these desires and then not give me someone to love."

"I have hated men since I was eleven years old. That's when my father started slipping into my bed at night to fondle me until he climaxed."

"I thanked God after I masturbated. I don't know what I would have done if I had not had that outlet."

"I've tried to stop having illicit sex. I know it's wrong, but the truth is, I'm so happy right now, I don't want to think about God."

"I want a man. I want marriage. But I've been so disappointed in the past, I don't know if I can ever completely trust a man again."

"For three years I've tried to give up my immoral sexual habits but I fail time and time again. I feel like such a hypocrite. Do you think I should stop coming to church?"

There *are* solutions for these women's problems. But they're not easy solutions. In Part 2, "Work, Money, and Things," we will examine our need for purpose and reevaluate how we handle our daily responsibilities. It is not uncommon for a woman to claim to be trusting God, when, in reality, she is refusing to take hold of her life. It concerns me to see:

the growing number of women over sixty-five who have not provided for themselves in any way whether married or single.

that most of the Christian single women I speak with have no consistent savings plan.

how many Christian women are dreadfully unhappy with their jobs and yet refuse to think through their situation logically.

how sinful passivity is misinterpreted as a Christian virtue.

how busyness and activity are misinterpreted as solutions to life's problems.

the common fantasy of many women, married and single, that around the corner "escape" is possible.

the refusal of many women to take responsibility for their own happiness, which then makes them feel trapped by their circumstances.

God has called us to be strong and resolute. When we are, we feel good. As we gain control of our work, money, and things, our lives become even greater gifts to the Father. In Part 3, "Beyond Singleness," we will discuss the hope, meaning, and purpose we single Christians have. My expectations for us are not low; they are high. My prayer for Christian single women is not that we simply feel better about being single, but that we lead lives that are genuinely useful to Jesus Christ.

We have a price to pay for becoming godly women. The price is to live with hearts that are merciful and sensitive to the struggle of the real world around us. The first two parts of this book may, at times, be painful to read. There's a reason for this. They're designed to help us face life, to cauterize our wounds, and to strip away the walls that surround our hearts. They're designed to set us free. Yet, if the first two parts are intended to help us face life, the third part, "Beyond Singleness," is designed to help us live life with abandon, to trust God in a way that we have never experienced before.

The Divine Paradox

You and I know that the Christian life holds both pain and joy. And I suspect that many times while reading this book you may wonder if you have what it takes to live a life that's genuinely different. Let me encourage you in this. Remember the miracle of the cross. The cross on which Christ died is also the sign that he rose again from the dead. We're not struggling alone. Christ walks with us. We stand by his grace.

The cross is not only a symbol of suffering but also a symbol of joy. This paradox is the mystery that has led Christians for two thousand years. Men and women, knowing both the difficulty and the joy of the cross, have not held back their hearts but have taken up the cross and have moved forward to change the world.

Christianity is nothing if it is not a miracle.

So we pray for ourselves a miracle: that the Holy Spirit will touch our imaginations, that we will receive a new vision of what it is to be obedient to God, that we will be irresistibly drawn to the Father where miraculous things do still happen—and it makes no difference whether we're married or single.

OUR SOURCE OF WHOLENESS

*I*f each of us has not only an emotional need for love but also a biological desire for sex and if God created men and women for each other, then the absence of a godly man in a woman's life is bound to be painful. Yet sometimes we fail to recognize this. We know we have desires, but we think because we're Christians these desires will eventually go away. Most of us feel we ought to be able to escape the pain of aloneness, but we can't figure out how. We try to adjust to a world that is blatantly sexual and a God who says, "Be still, and know that I am God" (Ps. 46:10). Caught between two worlds, we feel more like victims than victors.

When this happens, single women may wonder, can a woman be separated from her desire for love? Can a woman know the whole of the female experience if she has no sexual experience? Did God create her only to be part of a pair or did he create her for something else?

One woman said to me, "Gigi, tell the Christian single woman she can be whole without a man." Another angrily rebuffed, "How can I be whole when part of me is sitting on the shelf unused?" One woman wept quietly, "I know this is wrong, but sometimes I hate God. How could he create in me passion and desire, give me the ability to enjoy another person, without giving me someone to love and a release for my desire?"

We have difficulty seeing that God loves us when we spend so much of our time trying to escape the immediate pain of aloneness.

Part of our aloneness is due to our natural, biological urges. The sex drive is powerful. It was placed in us for a reason—procreation. But God also created sex for pleasure, to draw men and women toward each other in love. Sexual pleasure is one of the richest, most satisfying experiences men and women can share. We don't want to deny this, but we don't want to be fooled by it either.

The physical drive for sexual intimacy and the emotional need for love are two different things. Although they can be companions, *they also can be separated.* We won't die if we don't have sex. It's not like food or water. Without it we will not shrivel up and waste away. We will, however, have a noticeable change in our demeanor if we don't have love. It's crucial for all of us to learn to distinguish love from sex. If we don't we'll be swept away by the flood of propaganda unleashed on us daily.

You may respond, "So what? Even if we don't have sex, we still need love. But we don't have love either. No wonder we're lonely!" Let me share something with you that few people want to admit: no one gets the love he or she wants—not the married woman, the married man, the single woman, or the single man. Humanity has been so blighted by the Fall that perfect human love is no longer possible. It has been said that loneliness is the most commonly shared human experience. God's love is the only sure love any of us will ever know. The solution to human loneliness is reconciliation with the Father through Jesus Christ. This is our hope—the love and power of God, which overcomes the world, and even our loneliness.

Our Struggle for Fulfillment

We live in a tragically damaged world. The relationship between man and woman, created to be so fulfilling, has been distorted beyond recognition. Yet, we don't always trust the solution God has to offer. Unfortunately, we women often look for our identity and worth in this world of warped images.

When we push for worth and acceptance apart from God, we become confused. This confusion leads to an urgency to find our worth and acceptance. This urgency leads to restlessness. At that point, many of us turn to a readily available source of affirmation—men. Since our emotional need for men and our physical desire for them are very real, we may engage in behavior ranging from light flirtatious play to deep romantic fantasizing. The result of this behavior is powerful—we feel instant exhilaration, an emotional and biological high that immediately lets us know we're desirable as women. We mistake the sensation for identity and worth.

But sensuality is only one *expression* of our womanliness. It is not womanliness itself. If we don't recognize this, we won't be able to claim any identity without the presence of men. We will miss seeing what womanhood is, and we may miss being the whole women God wants us to be.

Not all women who are lonely turn to men. Some trust only themselves. Self-trust can be just as powerful as attraction to the opposite sex. It's possible for us to find a degree of worth and acceptance in our natural intellectual ability, creativity, physical beauty, individual temperaments, or energy levels; it's possible to find a degree of worth and acceptance in our God-given abilities without turning to God at all.

We can be Christians, successful, and fairly happy, yet still not be the women God has called us to be. We can fool ourselves and miss the deep warmth and peace that is ours when we allow Christ's love to lead us into wholeness.

Am I saying that to desire physical and emotional satisfaction is wrong, that to desire success and marriage is wrong? Am I saying that men and women should never have relationships or that we should never be happy in life? Absolutely not. Man-woman relationships are inevitable and it's normal to want to be happy. But I'm also saying that most of us could take a better way. Most of our loneliness is because we don't look to the better way—we are spiritually blind. Spiritual blindness produces two things in us. First, we don't see how good, good is, and, second, we don't see how bad, bad is. Let's take the blinders off our eyes so that we can see God's goodness.

Married but Lonely

We Christian single women often think we would not be lonely if we had mates, but marriage doesn't guarantee we won't be lonely. For example, a married woman might be frightened because she's suffering from poor health. She confides to her husband, "I'm scared, honey. I'm worried because this is happening." She longs for her husband to acknowledge her emotional need for his support and involvement. Instead the husband himself isn't whole in Christ and doesn't recognize his opportunity to meet his wife's need or, if he does, he backs away from it. "What are you worried about?" he says. "There's nothing to be afraid of."

What the wife wishes her husband would say to her is, "I'm here, and I care. I can't change your circumstances, but I'll lovingly support you as you're going through this experience. I'll try to help you deal with your feelings." Since he doesn't respond that way she doesn't have in her marriage the fullness God intended her to have. She feels a lack of wholeness, just as you or I do. She feels desperately alone.

Men, too, enter marriage with expectations. They, too, have hopes, longings, and desires. But because many women don't know how to be the women God intended them to be, their husbands are just as disappointed in marriage as they are. Their wives may be excellent household managers, good mothers, good sexual partners, but their unwillingness to meet their husbands' emotional needs leaves many men lonely too.

The fact is, apart from God's grace, men are not what God originally intended men to be and women are not what God intended women to be. Whether married or single, none of us can ever find wholeness in human companionship alone.

Is Woman Whole without a Man?

In understanding wholeness we need to start with creation. "God created man in His own image; in the image of God He created him; male and female He created them" (Gen. 1:27). The *him* in this passage is generic, referring not specifically to Adam or to men, but to the human race. The full expression of God's character in creation is both male and female. Women reflect the image of God in a way men do not. Men reflect the image of God in a way women do not. When Hosea described the child Ephraim as being soothed and comforted in God's arms, how womanly that is. When Scripture refers to God as our Shepherd, our Lord, and our King, how masculine that is. God expresses a unique part of himself in both maleness and femaleness.

God created man strong and decisive, able to take charge of life. Man was to be responsible to God for the direction of humanity. God created woman gentle, open, vulnerable, responsive to Adam's initiative.

God intended for man and woman to complement one another, to be companions to one another, to be a pair. Eve enjoyed the strength of her husband. Adam enjoyed the vulnerability of his wife. Together they enjoyed love, openness, and depth of relationship. Adam poured his life, his sperm, into his wife. Eve opened her heart, her loins, to her husband.

But in addition to love and pleasure, God intended for man and woman to share their labor and responsibility. Their sum total, their chief purpose, was to glorify God and enjoy him forever. Man and woman were to do what Christ did on the cross: to give themselves totally without holding back from God or from one another.

Do you begin to glimpse the goodness of what God created? Allow yourself to imagine a world where men and women interacted as God intended. There would be courtesy and consideration, protection and admiration, comfort and love.

Men and women have long since defiled the perfection of creation. Much of the pain of loneliness is caused by living in a fallen world. We need to learn to distinguish between these two types of pain. Worldly solutions to our lives intensify our pain and increase our loneliness. Christ's solution to our lives cures our pain and heals our fallen world.

We are all affected by the Fall, all crippled by the brokenness of the man-woman relationship. We all should weep over contention between the sexes, single parent households, every divorce.

So we go before Christ with these things and allow our hearts to be broken. We acknowledge to him and to ourselves how great our loss truly is. We allow ourselves to feel the pain that aloneness and a fallen world cause. We confess to the truth that woman is not whole without man, and man is not whole without woman. And none of us is whole without one man—Jesus Christ.

Hallelujah, a solution to our singleness! We may be lonely, but we're not alone. We have a God who loves us and can give us victory in our lives. Jesus Christ's death on the cross has made us whole. We may never stop having a certain social uneasiness about being single, but we can have a deep sense of personal wholeness. We can understand how very precious we are to our Lord. We can see how much he cares for us and can bathe in that love. That is true wholeness in the best sense of the word.

THE GAMES PEOPLE PLAY

*D*id you know that the most maddening thing each of us has to deal with here on earth is the fact that life and people aren't what they're supposed to be? Did you also know that it's okay to be mad, really mad, if we get mad at the same things that anger God? Anger over our own sin motivates us to change. Sometimes it takes anger for us really to see ourselves and trust our Father. Let's get mad. Something which is so good—the relationship between men and women—has been and is being destroyed by each of us. Because of our own sin and the brokenness of humanity, we're missing something good which God intends each of us to enjoy.

Look around you. What do you see? In almost any group of Christian single men and women, most of the women will be attracted to a few of the men. The men will either stand together or gravitate toward only a few of the women. What about the remaining men and women? Aren't they also God's children? Don't they also desire relationships? Aren't they also people of value?

Perhaps the following remarks sound familiar.

"Bev and I date, but she's just a friend." (They have gone out two or three times a week for the past five years.)

"I like Amy, but to tell you the truth, her looks don't turn me on." (So, he ignores her.)

"Bill calls me all the time, and sometimes we go out, but it will never go anywhere." (Bill is a mechanic.)

"Bob is so spiritual." (Bob is also extremely good-looking.)

We often look for characteristics in others that will make us winners or make us look good, ignoring the fact that God has called us to consider others better than ourselves (see Phil. 2:3), and causing each other tremendous hurt.

Mutual exploitation of men and women builds walls of fear between them. Yet, we see the same attitudes and behavior again and again. We Christians say that we want godly mates, but we do little to encourage one another to be godly men or women. Most of us want to have our own needs met at the least amount of risk to ourselves. We are seldom willing to prayerfully prepare ourselves to meet the needs of others. The following are better responses to the above situations.

"I have been dating Bev for five years. God, I think I'm afraid of intimacy. Give me the courage to let her go in love or risk having her know me in a deeper way."

"I like Amy. It's true her looks don't turn me on. Lord, how can I reach out to her without leading her on? Help us to be good friends in you."

"God, next time Bill calls, help me to value him for who he is and not what he does."

"Bob is so good-looking. God, does he feel used the way women do?"

When we have been the brunt of others' selfishness, when we have been used to meet other people's needs, we may panic about new relationships. Recalling what happened in the past, we fear—even expect—to be let down or disappointed in some way. No wonder we don't confidently set out to meet the needs of others; we have been so battered by not having our own needs appropriately met.

Jane is feeling a little down and unsure of her femininity. She decides to flirt with Bill. Bill is not her first choice as a man, but he's a nice guy, who seems to be genuinely interested in her, and she gives him her undivided attention. After several weeks Tom, a new Christian, comes to their Bible study.

Jane and Tom click, so she drops Bill.

They date nonstop for six or seven weeks. Although they don't have intercourse, they have become physically involved. One day without even the courtesy of a phone call, Tom drops Jane. Knowing a physical relationship will ultimately mean responsibility, he wants out.

Next week at the Bible study Tom begins to flirt with Lisa. Jane, feeling abandoned as well as guilty, returns to Bill.

Cathy is a solid sort of person. Over the years she has parlayed a good personality and the ability to be a friend into real popularity. Most of the church's single activities center around her house.

Cathy has a secret crush on David, who is good-looking and considered a catch by most women. By saying that they are just good friends, Cathy has ingratiated herself to him over the years. She performs little favors for him, cooking his favorite meals, helping him type his resumé, remembering *his* mother's birthday when he would have forgotten. At first David was uncomfortable with Cathy's "friendship" but admits it has been so pleasant and convenient he has become accustomed to it.

David uses Cathy's house to meet other women to date. He likes pretty women with a little bit of flash. Although Cathy feels truly hurt each time she sees David go out with another woman, she is able to comfort herself with the fact that he always comes back to her.

You may be thinking, "I'm certainly not a Jane or a Tom or a Cathy or a David." Are you sure? Our need for relationship is so intense it is often difficult to see ourselves clearly.

While some people engage in this kind of hurtful behavior in their quest to satisfy their need for love, others do relational damage by avoiding any kind of relationship at all.

Because of the anxiety built up from our past experiences, most Christian single men and women aren't able to meet one another on any kind of biblical basis. Our fear of relationships is legitimate. But if we continue to support one another only when it's safe or easy, or when it affirms us in a way that we think is acceptable, a vicious pattern begins: barriers go up between us—barriers of boasting, feigned spirituality, silliness, cockiness, even office work or careers—anything that keeps other people from knowing who we are so we won't get hurt.

What can we do about this?

First, we recognize how precious man-woman relationships are, and second, that they are in jeopardy. Then, knowing that God intended relationships between the sexes to glorify him, we can call on his power to help us do our part in changing the way things are. As godly women, we can make a difference!

What Is a Godly Woman?

Joe and I dated through high school and college. The thing I liked most about him was that he always seemed to know what to do—to make things right—to comfort me when I was distressed. But sometimes he needed me, too.

I remember one day, after we had been married several years, Joe came home from work and sort of fell apart. I got nervous and all upset and fell apart too. The next day, whatever was wrong at work evened out for Joe, but he never ever fell apart in front of me again. What my husband needed, though I didn't know it at the time, was a godly woman.

A godly woman is gentle. She is tender and affectionate, yet underlying her softness is a strength that comes from an unswerving trust in God.

Open and free, she is unencumbered by manipulative ploys. She states her desires and opinions confidently, knowing that she is a woman loved by God and is validated by that love. She's also meek in the best sense of the word. Bankrupt in spirit, she says to her Lord, "Thy will be done." She knows her need for God and depends on him alone to direct her life.

The godly woman is not quarrelsome or contentious. She stands for righteousness and is peaceful in all her ways. Understanding her own sinfulness, mourning over the baseness of her motives, she is careful to review all her plans with the Father.

From her relationship with God the godly woman gains the strength she needs to be truly loving to her brother. She is able to remain vulnerable to him regardless of his behavior toward her. When he withdraws or is careless with her feelings, she doesn't pout, nag, or manipulate him. She allows him to be himself. When he uses her love for his own needs or hurts, she doesn't try to control him defensively or pull away in fear. She remains open to him while gaining her strength from God.

The godly woman so depends on God to meet her needs that whether or not she is involved with a man in the type of relationship she desires, she is still able to support him in a godly way. She loves him. She knows God made men and women for one another.

Drawn from the Beatitudes

Few of us are like that. If men, in general, are afraid of relationships, women are afraid of not having the type of relationship that will support them in a fulfilling way. Much of our emotional energy is spent either in looking for relationships we think will satisfy us, or in avoiding the pain of relationships because we fear they won't.

Few of us are willing to wait quietly for what God has in store for us. Most of us want what we want *now*. We women want to feel safe. We want security. Deep down, most of us dread any really big surprises, so we spend much of our time trying to control our lives.

What happens when a woman meets a man she's attracted to? She senses there is something special about him. She feels that if she could just get closer to him, know him better, she would be satisfied. At the same time, however, something else stirs inside her—fear. She is reluctant to reveal herself for fear that he will eventually let her down—disappoint her.

In both instances, she's on target. Men do have a unique capacity to satisfy us, but they also have an enormous potential to bring us pain. Because we want the pleasure and not the pain, we try to control them. Because we want relationships, and there is no way we can guarantee safety in relationships, we either try to control men or try to control our lives and exclude them.

Being soft, open, and vulnerable means we surrender control. If we're tender and kind and do absolutely nothing to manipulate men to meet our needs, we surrender control. If men fail us, yet we love and trust them anyway, we surrender control.

God wants us to give up controlling our relationships. He wants us soft and nonprotective. He wants no safety in our lives, no security—because he wants us broken, leaning on him, vulnerable, and tender, so we're able to allow our brothers to support us in a godly way.

When we resist leaning on God, we're unable to have godly relationships.

Facing Ourselves

Deep down we don't believe there are men who are so godly they'll support our needs at the risk of being vulnerable themselves. We don't believe there are men who will love us more than their own bodies or egos. So we don't look for these qualities; we're not godly women looking for godly mates.

Instead, we look for characteristics in men which will give us a sense of fulfillment *now*, qualities which will meet our needs for relationships *today*. We use men. We use them to meet our immediate need for intimacy. We look for soft words, long looks, little favors, special attentions, anything that will make us feel closer to them.

We use men to vicariously give us status. We believe that if we're close to men who are important—important by our culture's standards—we're also important by association. We believe that men who have good looks, good jobs, or money have worth and can somehow pass their worth on to us.

We use men to help us escape from the pressures of everyday life. A date with a "dull" man seems better than

41

an evening at the laundromat. Fantasizing about the man in the next office is more fun than thinking about the work to be done in this office. We may even believe that marriage to an ungodly man is better than growing old alone. Each of us longs for someone to take us away from "all this."

No wonder men don't reach out to us. We don't really care about men for themselves. We're more interested in what they can do for us. Because of our fears and our desire to control men to meet our needs, we women are little help to them. Unknowingly, we put a lot of pressure on them *not* to be spiritual. We put pressure on men to perform according to *our* expectations rather than God's.

When men are anxious to have their own ego needs met and don't receive what it takes to *feel* important, they begin to feel threatened. This puts them on the defensive. Men have reason to fear us. We have shown by our actions, by our aloof withdrawal, and by our critical hearts, that we aren't easy to please. Actually, we often don't accept men as they are.

Man's Need for Affirmation

The average man is not looking for a godly mate either. He is looking for affirmation. There's nothing wrong with desiring approval, but men usually want it without deep involvement. They want strokes without strength. They want affirmation without being willing to put their emotional energies at the disposal of someone else.

In general men can meet their needs in counterfeit ways more easily than women can. Some men pour themselves into their work and isolate their wives. Some absorb themselves in gadgets—computers, boats, cars—and appear perfectly contented. Others indulge in meaningless flirtations or affairs, or in *Playboy* alone in their rooms, and never reach out for deep relationships. Still others lose themselves so fully in their political or theological positions that they have little left of themselves to give away.

Some men, whether they're married or single, meet their biological and emotional needs apart from deep relationships with women. A man can become chairman of the board, drive a Porsche, have a mistress on the side, and die almost happy. But, unknowingly, he will have missed the profound experience of deep, meaningful relationship with a woman.

The world has lied, and many men have believed it. In their effort to avoid the pain of deep relationships, men have either attempted to manipulate women at little risk to themselves or they have looked for fulfillment in something less complicated than we are.

What is so sad is that the affirmation most wanted by men is women who truly care about them for themselves. In our fear we often withhold this. And in men's fear of relationships they often miss receiving it when we've had the courage to care.

Since the core of men is their egos, and egos usually need success in some form, and since no one can ever guarantee success in relationships, men, more than women, are afraid to risk deep relationships. Each time a man measures his own adequacy by how a woman responds to him, she has the power to frustrate him. Because of this power, and the actual frustration he feels, it is genuinely difficult for him to remain supportive in a way that is satisfying to them both. Unless a man looks to God, the dissatisfaction continues—the man's need for strokes blocks the woman's getting to know who he really is. Her desire for a relationship at any cost blocks her getting to know the man completely.

What Is a Godly Man?

The godly man has the courage to go God's way, even when there may be no evidence of success. He depends solely on God's truth to direct his life and not on the affirmation of others to feel good about himself.

This man's genuine strength comes from his faith in God. Yet he doesn't have trouble getting in touch with his own dependency.

He knows God has placed him on earth to rule, to be decisive, to decide the direction of humanity. Yet he also knows that there are few easy answers, that most of the decisions he must make lie in life's gray areas. So he decides with a difference—with a broken spirit. Seeing the wretchedness of his own heart, his ego, and his pride, he rejects masculine one-upmanship, game playing, or looking out for number one. He chooses, rather, the path of true sanctification: absolute helplessness before God.

That doesn't mean that the godly man is a namby-pamby. Far from it. Using Christ as his example, he takes hold, takes risks, and moves himself and others in the direction of God.

The godly man is supportive of woman. He doesn't measure his own worth by her response, and as a result, he is able to remain supportive when she has had a bad day, doesn't look so great, or is in a bad humor. He sees himself as valuable apart from woman, just as he expects woman to see herself as valuable apart from him. He knows that God made them interdependent creatures. So he reaches out when woman is afraid, comforts when she is down, leads when she is confused, and takes hold when she is distressed. The godly man does this because he knows woman needs him. He knows they were made for each other.

Drawn from the Beatitudes

We may never know any perfect men or be perfect women, but we can ask God to make us into the people he wants us to be. Such growth is within our grasp and God is longing to help us achieve it. By looking critically at the tragic lack of loving relationships between men and women, we can sense our need for God and turn to him. We can turn from our own sin while at the same time not letting men's sins affect us. By recognizing how good God's standards are and how far we fall short of them, we can choose to move toward God's standards. We can be the godly men and women he has called us to be.

20/20
VISION

*H*allelujah! God has not left us to our own devices. He has reached down to us in love. The relationship between men and women can be redeemed. Christ came not only to save us, but to give us power, to enable us to change, to make us more like him. "But we all, with unveiled face, beholding as in a mirror the glory of the Lord, are being transformed into the same image from glory to glory" (2 Cor. 3:18). This is our hope. As the Holy Spirit works within us, we are able to break the cycle of self-centeredness.

When we develop a vision of what it is to be godly, we see the image of a woman who is willing to be open and gentle and a man who is willing to be strongly involved at whatever level is appropriate. This vision will be so appealing to us that we won't be tempted to spoil it with destructive behavior. Instead, we'll want to concentrate on building godly relationships.

What Are Godly Relationships?

Godly relationships are those between men and women who honor the other above themselves. They lay down their lives, sacrifice their own desires, and do what is genuinely best for their brothers or sisters regardless of their own feelings. This is not always easy, but it is necessary for godly relationships.

Godly relationships begin with ourselves. We relax, look to Christ, and realize how really helpless we are apart from him—how defensive and layered with self-protection we are. By looking to Christ for our security we are able to avoid the self-protective behavior patterns we have developed over the years. We turn from the tendency to manipulate in order to gain intimacy. We risk rather than insist on security and safety. We stand alone rather than do anything ungodly for affirmation.

Then, because Christ loves us "anyway," with all our imperfections, we can love our brothers "anyway," too. We can stop looking at them as objects which, because of our fears, we must either reject or conquer. Instead, we can look at them as men who are in our lives for a purpose. As we begin to see our own lives as having meaning to God, we begin to see their lives this way also.

As we look to God for our strength and joy, it will be easier for us to let go of our desire to control men. We will be able to let down our barriers and allow our brothers to take charge in a godly way. What happens when they disappoint us? When they fail—and they will fail time and time again—we look to God for our security and not to our brother. When we fail—and we will—they must look to God for affirmation and not to us. As we and they repeat this process, we will all grow stronger: they not in their need for affirmation from us, but in their strength from God; we not in our need for security from our brothers, but in our dependency upon Christ. The result is *whole* people, godly men and godly women, able to reach out and engage in pure relationships.

A Godly Woman in an Ungodly World

The women who desire to be godly women in an ungodly world are willing to be fully women, whether men are willing to be fully men or not. This means she can enter into fellowship with her brothers in Christ whole before God at whatever level is appropriate for the individual relationships because her relationships with men are based on her knowing her own value to God and her worth in Jesus Christ. This enables her to respond to her brothers with feminine warmth and acceptance, given the parameters of the relationships. An appropriate closeness is possible between a single man and a single woman or a married man and a single woman or a single man and a married woman because of Jesus Christ.

We can be fully female with male shopkeepers and fully female with our boyfriends. Our association with each is different, but we can be completely godly women with both. Unfortunately, because we aren't always sure of our worth as persons, we aren't sure of ourselves as women. Because we aren't sure of our real value to God, we miss a variety of relationships and we keep ourselves from each other.

If we want to move toward godly relationships with men, the key is to yield our womanliness to Christ as faithful stewards of everything he has given us. Once we accept the fact that God truly loves us, we will also be able to accept our femaleness. This keeps us in touch with our hearts, which keep us in touch with our Father.

Then we can confidently deal with the variety of relationships that exist between single men and women. Acquaintance is one.

Acquaintance

Male acquaintances add zest to our lives. We all know men who may not be our friends or our romantic ideals, but our lives are made richer because of them. It's okay to offer a glass of water to the UPS man, smile at the man you see every day in the elevator, help the bagboy put the groceries in your car, or ask your boss if he had a nice holiday.

We can give to our male acquaintances a pleasant, warm demeanor and a genuine concern for them. As acquaintances we can utilize the first and easiest way we have of enjoying people for who they are—of allowing them to feel and experience their worth to God.

If what we desire is pleasant association with other human beings, then we maintain gentle, open, nondefensive attitudes toward our male (and female) acquaintances. We enjoy them for *who* they are; we pay attention to them because we're genuinely interested in them; we realize that God values them, just as he values us.

We can be friendly and sincere without suggesting familiarity. But if an acquaintance does mistake our intentions, we remember that we are on our Father's business. We firmly end the conversation and walk away. Being fully feminine does not mean being a marsh-mallow. It simply means being women wholly open to God, and as a result, open and kind to the men in our lives.

Friendship

Friendship has its own special chemistry. It is more a bond of love than a sexual pull. A friendship is characterized by a genuine concern for the other's well-being, a willingness to sacrifice on the other's behalf. A mutual interest—a hobby, sport, or goal—may launch a friendship. Or it may be that friends simply grew up in the same neighborhood, attend the same church, work in the same place.

Whatever it is that unites people, true friendship involves mutual give and take and open encouragement.

One thing we want to watch out for in male-female friendships is that we don't play with each other's emotions in a selfish way. A lot goes on under the name of friendship that is not friendship at all.

Some men are threatened by any relationship with a woman, so they flirt to satisfy their egos and call it friendship because it's easier for them to handle. This, of course, is not friendship at all. It's taking advantage of a woman's openness and it is quite painful at the time. If you desire to be a true friend to such a man, you might want to explain to him that you enjoy him as he is, that flirting is unnecessary, and that you believe your friend-ship will grow genuinely deeper without it. If this causes him to back off, keep reaffirming him as a man and as a good friend. Allow him to know how really valuable he is.

Another situation to watch out for in male-female friendships is using our male friends to satisfy the need to have men in our lives at any cost. In this situation we ask ourselves why the presence of men is so necessary for our self-worth. Although there will always be a certain male/femaleness in any relationship between sexes, we should not unfairly lead men on. Men have feelings just as we do. We want to build healthy relationships, not destroy them. Friendship is the basis for all good interaction.

A true friendship between man and woman does not come along every day; however, it is one of the richest relationships possible. It is worth working on and worth the risk of involvement.

The Date

Dating is fun, but in my opinion, the system is false. It does not exist in most cultures of the world, but since it does here, we need to know how to deal with it.

Quite often the date is a setup for emotional and sexual frustration. Many men and women who date are not looking at an acquaintance or even a friend to see if it is God's will that the association be carried further into a love relationship. Rather, they are looking for instant affirmation, and they use dating as a tool. Others are horribly excluded by the dating system. Unless dating is used as a serious step to examine the possibility of further commitment, the whole process is premature, and, if sensuality is involved, dangerous.

In traditional dating, the man invites the woman, the man pays. The woman waits, the man approaches. The man anticipates the woman's desires, the woman desires to please.

In order to be proper stewards of our sensuality, a good rule is: if in doubt, don't date. Keep these relationships with men at a friendship level. He pays, you pay. He makes suggestions, you make suggestions. He's helpful, you're helpful. Dating has ruined many potentially good love relationships by rushing couples past the getting to know one another stage and into the physically intimate stage.

Dating is the time to begin preparing for love relationships, to examine our thinking. We must depend on Christ for our fulfillment and respect our dates' opinions, ideas, and beliefs. If you find that you and the man you are dating differ in lifestyles and beliefs, have the courage to back off lovingly and firmly. Respect both his value as a person and God's will. If the man backs off from you and it hurts too much, consciously force yourself to relax and to realize the support of God's love. Although broken relationships always hurt to a certain extent, it's good to examine your motives—to ask yourself what you were expecting from this relationship. Were you looking to the man and not to Christ for fulfillment?

I cannot emphasize enough the satisfaction that comes from having a godly, non-manipulative relationship with a man, to desire his well-being as much as your own.

Fool's Love

Fool's love is like fool's gold. When we *so* desire earthly love that we put that desire *before* our sensitivity to the Lord's leading, we fall into fool's love. In today's world of easy accessibility to one another and with its emphasis on instant solutions, it is not uncommon for a man and a woman to be acquaintances one week and to fall into fool's love the next.

If a woman is attracted to a man, her desire to be loved becomes more urgent, and a romantic aura can flame quickly and burn brightly. Romance can be marvelous. Songs are written about it; poems immortalize it. It just plain feels good. But romance can also be a two-edged sword. If we don't think clearly, we can be fooled.

Because of our desire for excitement (our hearts beat faster), for status (to be loved by men we think are important), for escape (men to think about and be with apart from our humdrum routines), we will do almost anything to keep these satisfactions coming. At this point we must proceed carefully and prayerfully. It is here that Satan can most easily fool us. God created man and woman to glorify himself. A victory for Satan can result when we allow our psychological needs and biological urges to push us into relationships that will not glorify God or be lasting for the participants. Many have married with only fool's love as a basis. They did not prepare themselves or wait for what God had in mind for them.

Love

Real love between man and woman is as romantic and exciting as fool's love but it is more: it is a gift from God. God's love is the model of human love. We see examples in his love for the nation Israel and in Jesus' love for the church.

One aspect of real love is elasticity. It is ever-growing, ever tolerant. It is flexible enough to encompass the variety of moods of two people in a relationship. Real love isn't always easy and it doesn't always feel like love. However it's worth the time and patience it takes to develop it.

Nowhere in Scripture do we read, "Wives love your husbands." We do read, "Husbands love your wives." Wives are to revere, submit to, respect their husbands. When a man is strongly supportive in a relationship, willing to take hold in a meaningful way, love follows. When a woman is gentle, open, vulnerable, she responds in love.

Unlike the women who are married because they fell for fool's love, many women are single today because they're afraid of real love. They're afraid to risk, to relinquish control, to give themselves completely to another. Part of this fear is a reaction to all the fool's love we see, but part of it is because we have not developed our capacity to love wholly. Whether we're married or single, we all want to have the *capacity* to love. We want love and marriage to be a choice, not something that escapes us or is denied us because of our fears. As Christian single women we want to become so capable of loving, so giving, that should godly men never be available to us, should we never participate in a specific, loving relationship, we can still give the love we have freely to others.

Beloved sisters, we want to be women who, although we may hurt, although we may feel empty, although we may be lonely, are still able to reflect the love of God in our ability to love.

The Gift of Celibacy

If we are ever to have the gift of celibacy, and not just celibacy itself, it will come from our ability to love freely. From genuine hurt and disappointment, we are touched by God and rise up beautiful. There is something unexplainable within us—an ability to love that goes beyond self-interest, a supernatural love as deep and fulfilling as married love.

We have a gift called the "firstfruits to God and to the Lamb" (Rev. 14:4). It is a gift that the apostle Paul referred to as "good" (1 Cor. 7:1) and for many centuries was considered a higher calling than marriage. With this gift of celibacy we can attend the Lord without distraction; we have a passion that surpasses that of eros.

The gift of celibacy has been devalued through the church's neglect of the subject; a disservice has been done to single Christians. Yet this reticence is understandable. We find it hard to tackle the subject because we often equate the gift of celibacy with celibacy alone.

How many of us have known Christian men or women who were celibate but were miserable creatures to be around? The lack of a specific human love made their lives loveless. God's *gift* of celibacy, however, has just the opposite effect. It makes those who have it more loving.

Many Christian single women today are celibate and hate it. Hanging on by their fingernails or else hardened by a sense of rejection, they are afraid to ask for the gift of celibacy. They believe praying for such a gift would lock them into a life of even more strain or isolation.

God's command for sexual purity and chastity is an absolute for all Christian single people. It does not vary. Yet the gift of celibacy is a specific gift from the Father. To pray for the gift of celibacy is to pray for the ability to accept chastity, for the ability to channel love to others, to be at ease with singleness.

Not having mates does not mean we're sentenced to lead loveless lives. It means that we have no one else to depend on but the Father. In our aloneness we have the opportunity to deepen our relationship with him and to love more broadly than we could as married women. We have an opportunity to take what the world sees as a "tragedy" and "impossibility" and glorify the Father.

This is what we are called to do.

Without God and the gift of his love, celibacy is really rather sad. But with God and his gift of love, we can enjoy a life alone.

STEWARDSHIP OF SEXUALITY

*H*ow we understand our sexuality is basic to how we as single women manage it in our lives. In earlier chapters you read statements reflecting the natural pain of aloneness some Christian women feel. At times we do feel pain, yet we can faithfully turn to Christ and determine to do nothing which is neurotic or sinful. God knows this. If you respond this way, good—you need not be burdened to change. Other of the comments you read, however, reflected warped thinking and ungodly expectations. Our sexuality combined with our backgrounds, circumstances, and the influences of society have damaged our thinking to an unbelievable extent. The results have had a detrimental effect on our lives. This may have happened beyond our control and without our even realizing it.

Much of the pain and unhappiness we feel is a result of these wrong beliefs rather than God's design for our lives. To determine whether we are caught in a maze of wrong thinking, let's examine what sexuality really means.

First we need to recognize that all women are sexual beings. Our physiological response to sexual attraction is not a choice; it's a fact. It's not as if we're sexual when we have sex but are made of cardboard when we don't. God created us with sexuality and it is good. But he wants us to express it in our lives as he intended. How we do this is where much of the confusion arises. To have victory in our stewardship of sexuality we first need to believe genuinely that God's design for sexuality makes sense.

God created men and women to be drawn together in love. This love is to be culminated by sexual union, which in marriage is a good thing. As single Christian women, however, we need to believe that for those of us who are not able or who choose not to marry, God has made available the gift of celibacy. We respond to a different calling—*chastity in obedience to God.*

Once we intellectually understand the goodness of what God has designed, we will stop assuming that sexuality is something which, if not expressed, will make us either dreadfully unhappy or dreadfully unfulfilled. Instead, we can begin to think of sexuality as one aspect of womanhood which, if not expressed, we may miss but which will not keep us from being fully woman. We can still be whole.

When this is established in our minds, we can then choose not to go in the direction of the world, but in the direction of God. This won't be easy, but the struggle with obedience to God will give us a deeper understanding of what it means to be a woman. We will know more as a result of our efforts than we can learn from any magazine article, TV talk show, or treatise on women.

In our surrender to Jesus Christ, we are women who do not repress our sexuality but who acknowledge it and are good stewards of it.

Suppression Vs. Repression

To suppress means consciously to choose to control certain of the very real emotions or thoughts we experience. To repress them is to exclude them unconsciously from the conscious mind.

A stimulus may arouse sexual excitement in a woman, but after acknowledging that these desires exist, she can then choose not to indulge in fulfilling these desires. This is suppression and it's good.

If, however, a sexual stimulus engages a woman and rather than acknowledging its effects she denies them—perhaps because of fear or a previous negative experience—that's repression, and it's bad.

In order to be proper stewards of our sexuality we learn to suppress and, at the proper time, within God-given parameters, to express our sexuality. We should never repress or deny our sexuality.

But, you may ask, why not? If we can't have sex, at least if we repress our desires we don't feel anything, and that seems good. The problem with repressing our desires is that when we deny our natural sexual responses, we run the risk of denying other responses, too. Whenever we deny anything created by God, something happens inside us. In the case of repression, we become disengaged—withdrawn. A wall goes up between us and those around us. Then it may make no difference to whom we're relating; we'll have already distanced ourselves from them.

It's true that by repressing a desire we don't feel the pain of it, but we don't feel its pricks of tenderness either. When we try, for any reason, to escape the reality of the Fall, when we deny the pain of life and the fact that the world is not what it should be, when we refuse to suffer as Christ suffered, we forfeit the compassion and the love that Christ had. We miss the tenderness that is possible for us to have for one another.

While many women are hopping in and out of bed for the wrong reasons, other women are avoiding good and godly relationships and even remaining single for the wrong reasons. Proper stewardship of our sexuality means to be fully sexual and yet to choose, because of our belief in the validity of God's way, to be in charge of the feelings God has given us.

Romantic Imagery

Imagination and daydreams have a purpose in God's plan for relationships. Romantic imagery can be good. For example, we can talk to our male friends in church and enjoy the essence of male-female relationships. We can think about what it would be like to talk to this man again. This is fine, unless our interest in them as persons is overpowered by our desire to have our own needs met through them.

Unfortunately, this sometimes happens. We see men in church, talk to them, enjoy the thought of a male-female relationship, and we go a little crazy. We don't stop to think about how we can love these men as our brothers in Christ; we begin to think about how they can meet *our* needs and how they can fit into *our* plans for *our* lives.

This is what I call larger-than-life romantic fantasizing. Romantic fantasies look innocent on the outside, but they're a particularly insidious way of robbing men of their maleness by predetermining what we want them to be. We don't accept them as they are.

Men are fragile creatures just as we are. How much more loving on our parts if we accept them as they are, without fantasizing about what we want them to be.

How dehumanizing for the average man when he meets a woman who has just been fantasizing about "the man of her dreams"!

The larger-than-life romantic fantasy does not build relationships, it destroys them. If our dreams are "better" than real life, we don't come to terms with the difficulty of real relationships. To be proper stewards of our sexuality, we can enjoy romantic imagery within the framework of relationships, but we must be careful to see men in human terms. Only then can we love them with the love of God and build solid relationships with them in Christ.

Masturbation

Masturbation is the sexual response to self-stimulation. The sensual response to touch is a good thing. Whether it is to be enjoyed alone is a question you must decide. Scripture is silent on the subject of masturbation. Scripture is not silent, however, on the subject of lust which is an intense desire for the forbidden and is against the will of God.

Generally speaking, masturbation is accompanied by lustful fantasies. Like the larger-than-life romantic fantasy, lust uses our brothers for our own gratification. The truth is that lust excites our passion, rather than quenches it, and once set in motion it's difficult to control. If not restrained, lust may manifest itself in such overt expressions of sexuality as sexual aggressiveness, manipulative flirting, or at times, a search for a sexual partner for release. If lust does not find release in an overt expression, it will find it in a passive form such as masturbation.

Shere Hite, in her reports on male and female sexuality, observes that many of the men and women she interviewed experienced more intense physical pleasure in masturbation than in coitus with their partners. Men and women had more intense physical pleasure *alone* than with one another. This fact has nothing to do with our consideration of the wrongness or rightness of masturbation, but ironically, it points up a truth about sexual union as God intends it: intercourse requires the participants to know one another fully. It takes communication, time, patience, and love. Without these, engaging in sex does not fully satisfy, as many are discovering.

If sexually active men and women have discovered the need for emotional intimacy as well as physical intimacy, the celibate woman must recognize it twofold. Yet if we think of our sexuality only as the immediate gratification of pleasurable impulses, if we put no emphasis on relationships and ministry to one another, we will have missed the boat. Then we, like the people interviewed by Ms. Hite, will find masturbation more satisfying than interaction with our brothers.

Masturbation, like alcohol and drugs, is a form of escape. It is not unusual for a woman with tension in another area of her life to try to escape in masturbation. Let me suggest something I have discovered to be true. When I desire a true relationship with a man, when I seek to minister to his needs and am completely woman with an openness that is appropriate in the context of our relationship, I find that although the physical aspect of a relationship is absent, the other is so satisfying I have less desire for the physical. I have a genuine desire to rightly manage my sexuality and protect the man's as well.

Lesbianism

It is good for Christian women to love one another, to comfort one another, to be affectionate, to laugh together, to embrace, to kiss one another on the cheek in friendship. But these actions do not mean the same things to all women.

Some women, because of their backgrounds, because of misinformation and experiences from the past, have diverted their attention from men to women. Intense fear has blocked their desire for men. Because of this fear, and because they have a natural desire for love, these women have substituted an unnatural desire for their sisters.

Women who have lesbian tendencies know it. Sometimes the feeling is mild and experienced occasionally. They may feel it in connection with one person and never experience it again. However, for most women who struggle with lesbianism, it is an intensely painful and ongoing experience. Homosexuality, expressed sexuality with a partner of the same sex, is a sin.

Let me express my love as an outpouring of God's love to the woman who suffers from these desires. I want you to know there is no sinful desire from which God does not offer an avenue of escape. I want to give you hope in your ability, through Christ's power, to change your unnatural desires to natural ones. I want to give you hope in your ability to love, if not a specific man, then to love the world in a significant way.

If you struggle with such tendencies and have not already contacted a Christ-centered pastor or priest, I suggest that you do so. You might also want to see a Christian counselor. In either case, be specific about your goal: you need to expect counsel in turning from this sin, not in adjusting to it.

Flirting

Flirting—playfulness, eye contact, and the like—is an overt expression of sexuality. It says to another person, "I'm interested." One only has to look at the animal kingdom to see demonstrations of flirtatiousness. The head nodding of the crane and the foot stomping of the bull work fine for the animals. Unfortunately, humans are not so direct in communicating their signals. In an attempt to get our needs met at the least risk to ourselves, we're inclined to send out false signals or self-centered messages. These overt expressions of sexuality which were meant to give the other gender clues of our intent are used instead to manipulate for strokes or to gain control in a situation.

Sometimes a woman is so anxious to satisfy her social needs—to obtain a date, a husband, or a better position at work—that flirtatiousness is not a sensual matter at all. In these cases it is not used for sexual enjoyment or to communicate interest, but rather to manipulate men.

Flirtation not only involves sending signals; it also involves receiving them. One researcher observed that in flirting some who may be interested in developing relationships will behave in a negative manner, causing crucial key communication to go wrong, thus actually impeding the possibility of future relationships.[2] In other words we are often so self-conscious we miss the opportunity to flirt!

In a proper stewardship of our sexuality with regard to flirtation we should seek openness, truth, and responsibility: openness to our own feelings and the feelings of others; truth in examining our false views of life so that we're careful in what we are communicating; and responsibility to men so as not to lead them on unfairly. Remember, it's important to learn not only how to give signals, but to be sensitive enough to receive them.

Kissing

Of the two types of kisses, the social kiss and the sensual kiss, we are concerned here with the sensual kiss—the one most misunderstood.

A friend of mine, a beautiful woman who dropped out of the jet set of Palm Beach when she accepted Christ, put it this way: "I don't kiss. Kissing is foreplay. If I don't like the man, I don't want that type of intimacy with him. If I do, it leads to something more, which is either guilt-producing or frustrating."

The sex act seldom begins in the bedroom. It begins with a light touch on the arm, a stroke of the hair, a kiss. How beautiful is the rhythm of love, but we must understand that it is just that—rhythm designed for conclusion in coitus. The kiss is not something to regard lightly.

Biological reactions and emotional needs urge us toward one another. This is fine if we are preparing ourselves for godly love, but I would venture to say that, for most people, this is not usually the case. In today's culture a kiss is often expected as a matter of course between a couple at the end of an evening. The kiss is used as a sign of acceptance, a way of saying, "I don't reject you." The kiss is used as a weapon in the power struggle of the sexes. It is often deceitful.

The kiss can be deceptive because the touching and caressing awake biological urges that mask and confuse true feelings and prevent God-centered relationships. Once begun by a simple, innocuous kiss, the resulting feelings may become overpowering. Many women and men do not know their own minds in the midst of a tender embrace.

It is important to know your mind *before* you kiss. A woman who desires to be a good steward of her sexuality should ask herself, "Why?" when she is thinking about kissing a man. Is it because she's afraid of hurting the man's feelings if she doesn't kiss him? She must think of another way to affirm him as a man. Is it because she thinks it's expected of her at the end of the evening? She must stand up against a social system that perpetuates this idea. Is she thinking of kissing him because she wants power? Does she simply enjoy the feeling that a man desires her? That power will dull her sensitivity to her own needs as well as to the needs of the man.

Is she thinking of kissing the man because she wants love? The most dangerous reason of all is to kiss because we "want love." We kiss because we love, not because we want love. Such self-centeredness is one of the main barriers that keeps us from getting to know the men we kiss.

In the wise stewardship of our sensuality, a kiss is pleasant but it also has meaning. It never communicates nothing.

Intercourse

The physical oneness of a man and a woman within the framework of marriage is good. Scripture is filled with sexual imagery that extolls intercourse. In Ephesians 5:23–30, Christ's love for the church is described as that between a husband and wife, as a model for human love in the context of marriage.

Unfortunately, men and women often want this highest form of intimacy outside the intended parameters of marriage. The sins of adultery and fornication are not uncommon today. For some of us, it's easier to be physically close than to be verbally or emotionally close.

It's easier to touch than to talk. It's easier to direct our own relationships than to bring our needs to God. Rather than look to God for guidance on how to serve, cherish, and communicate with one another, we try to find immediate release of our desires and frustrations. Rather than work toward a godly union in marriage, the complete union of body, mind, and soul in knowing love, we turn to shallow sex, intercourse that satisfies the physical urges alone. Misuse of sexuality denies the goodness of what God has for us.

Deep inside each of us is a fear of being known and of being found inadequate, but the anticipation of sexual intimacy drives us to reveal ourselves to one another. The pleasure of sexual attraction creates an atmosphere of mutual acceptance. Without the sweet satisfaction of sexuality, many men and women might never take the risk of having a true relationship.

It is true that sex outside of marriage can produce some pleasure and a temporary sense of well-being, but outside the boundaries of marriage and a godly love, it also produces a fear that isolates.

Because intercourse outside of marriage is not the will of God, misuse of sexuality in either fornication or adultery is self-defeating. It does not cure our loneliness; it intensifies it. This intensified loneliness makes us reach out for even more of the same release—more sex. Soon even this does not satisfy us, so that even in the most intimate relationship with another person, we are still desperately alone.

Chastity

Chastity fuels the gift of celibacy. It is good. What a tragedy that we have to hear about its virtues first on the Phil Donahue show and in our newspapers.

People in the secular world have learned through the abuse of sexuality the benefits of chastity. As a result of misuse of the man-woman relationship, with its emptiness and pain, they have come to realize that chastity is good. They have discovered what the church has always known, but because they have found it outside the Christian context, because we have lacked the courage to lead them in this discovery, they have found it without Christ's love.

Now we Christian women have the opportunity to tell secular women the real meaning of chastity, which results in the gift of celibacy. We can explain that as Christians we have the same tender emotions and desires, the same capacity to feel deeply, but that we have chosen to offer our painful emotions to our Lord. Our chastity is a sacrificial gift to him. In the words of King David we say, "nor will I offer burnt offerings to the LORD my God with that which costs me nothing" (2 Sam. 24:24).

A gift that costs us nothing is worth nothing. But when we know who we are, know our value, and understand the goodness of sensual pleasure and what we are missing and choose to offer it to our Lord anyway, he will not allow such a gift to go unnoticed. He will honor it in eternity, if not sooner. That is really good news to tell our secular sisters.

What Happens When We Fail?

I fail repeatedly in the stewardship of my sexuality and by continuing to manipulate men for attention and affection. Perhaps some of you fail too.

We want to respond, "Oh, well, I've failed but God's grace is sufficient." God's grace *is* sufficient, but anytime we have a glib reaction to sin we badly misunderstand

God's grace. God expects us to struggle against sin, to fight and not to give up. He expects us to repent.

True repentance starts with mourning which leads to spiritual power. We mourn over our failures and the perfection of God that escapes us. We mourn because the permissive society of the last twenty years has contributed to our weakness. We mourn because of the tension we feel. We want to be godly, but even so, we don't want to give up the sin we believe we need.

I cannot tell you how many times I have lain across my bed and wept, saying, "Lord, where is your power? Why am I this way?" when I know I'm this way because I'm a sinner. We are *all* "this way." None of us has what it takes to be godly apart from Christ. It is this realized sense of inadequacy that has marked the Christian saints over the centuries. C. S. Lewis said, "No man knows how bad he is until he has tried very hard to be good."[1] At this point we're on the verge of power. J. N. Darby used the illustration of the prodigal son, who, when he was hungry went to the pigsty for husks. When he was starving, he went to his father's house. That's the way of true repentance!

When we're just "kind of" hungry, when we're just "kind of" sorry we sinned, we try self-control, positive thinking, reading our Bibles just a little more, and we wonder why we don't have power. When we're desperate, we go to our Father and humbly ask him for grace. In absolute helplessness before God we find the power that changes us. We become dead to sin and alive to Christ.

Double Seduction

Satan tricks us in two ways: through our bodies and through our minds. Satan wants us to believe that we can handle situations we simply cannot handle. In sexuality, a certain distance must be maintained because of biology.

But Satan also tricks us in our minds. He tells us we cannot be whole without men—that we'll shrivel up and be frustrated, sex-starved old maids if we don't find fulfillment in specific love relationships. This simply is not true. We must not make the mistake of assuming that if we are never able to express physical love we cease to be fully woman. We are fully woman when we are open and loving, and when we live our lives the way God has called us to live them.

To you who are involved in inappropriate sexual relationships, I understand the deep feelings of frustration you feel—wanting to be obedient to God yet still wanting a love that is available now. However, when we live with unchecked sexual expression, we live at that level of gratification. If we can go beyond the idea that we "need" immediate gratification and accept the absence of legitimate pleasure, we open ourselves up to an even deeper love for Christ.

You might say, "But you don't know how hard I've tried to stop doing this or that." I'm sure you have. I've tried hard too. But when I *just* grit my teeth and say I'm not ever going to do this again, I'm likely to wind up doing it. Gritting your teeth and gutting it out alone usually will not work for a very long time. It takes Christ showing us how to get our thinking in godly order.

We always do what we *think* will work for us. When we sin sexually, we do so because we think that somehow this sin is going to work for us. We need to change our thinking to "God's way makes sense." Overcoming our desires is a battle, but we aren't fighting it alone. We have our Lord to sustain us and give us power.

We may conquer one sin only to find another, but power comes in the struggle. The Christian life, until the day we're made perfect by Christ's return, is a life of rhythm between wretchedness and grace. Like a child learning to ride a bicycle, we wobble, we twist, we weave down the path. We even fall off and skin our knees. But if we keep on trying, eventually we learn to ride. We learn to keep our balance and soon we know the exhilaration of pedaling through the countryside, the joy of a newly learned behavior.

We discover that we are not neurotic women taunted by the world. We are free women. We are women with a choice, and our choice is God.

PART TWO

WORK, MONEY, & THINGS

For it is God who works in you both to will and to do for His good pleasure. (Phil. 2:13)

WOMAN'S WORK

A recent article in the *Wall Street Journal* began this way:

> She sits in front of a diploma that says Radcliffe and behind a nameplate that says "Editorial Assistant." It is getting late, and she is getting tired. Her secretary went home three hours ago, and her dinner date has given up. The page of copy that she's proofing isn't very stimulating; she vaguely suspects that the graphs her secretary mocked up today were more interesting to work on. For that matter, she vaguely suspects that her secretary makes more than she does. But, she reflects, as she sips from a cold cup of coffee, she is lucky, isn't she? She's got a dream job in a glamour industry. And aren't commitment and dedication required when you have not just a job, but a career?[1]

When a woman pushes to succeed, she often questions her own femininity. She may even hold back her performance so as not to seem "unfeminine." As if that weren't bad enough, the overall pay for a woman is appalling. She's likely to be paid 20 percent less than her male equivalent ten years after graduating from college.[2]

The Christian woman who has to work to survive is often torn. She may object to the strident demands of feminists, yet the insensitivity of employers and clients is often demeaning. Not everyone can work for a "good boss." If she steps down, ten more women are waiting to take her place. If she moves up, she wonders who she is, how she got there, and how long she can keep up the pace. In the middle of the night she may think, "Surely this is not what God intended."

Defining Our Terms

Secular opinions and our own wrong beliefs have given us an unhealthy view of work. Whether we're materialists or antimaterialists, incredibly successful professionals or self-styled dropouts, the world sees us in terms of what we *do*. What is tragic is that we're never sure if what we *do* is enough. It's like being seated in a fancy restaurant, not knowing if we have enough money to pay the bill.

I'm using the phrase "woman's work" in this chapter because I would like to avoid the connotations of the word *career*. I want to avoid identifying Christian women by what we do and look at what we are called to be. I want to be very clear on this. I'm not against women's having careers, making money, or doing anything else in this world that we can do in a godly way, but I want us to know exactly what we're discussing. You see, I believe we allow our culture to manipulate the way we think about our labor, just as those in the secular world have.

Because of the hype of the media and the neglect of the church, we have distorted something ordained by God to be part of the very essence of humanity. We have taken our work, which is central to our lives, and made it much more complicated than it need be.

Udo Middleman, in his book *Pro-Existence,* observes that labor is a necessary part of expressing who we are. It is a matter of man's being. I'm sure he would agree that work is also the essence of woman's being.

Many Christians, me included, say that Christ is the center of our lives, but often our actions don't bear this out. We separate our activities into various unrelated packages which we tag *work, church, family, personal maintenance,* and *leisure.* Then, to make it worse, we further label these activities *Christian* or *secular.* It's as if Christ can have our lives overall, but our many detailed activities have our time. This fragmentation of our time and activities exhausts us.

When we hear people say they've turned their work over to God, what are they implying? They are implying that work does not fall into the realm of the Savior. When we talk of "taking God into the marketplace," what do we mean? We mean that God is not already in the work world. An insidious separation of Christ from our work has crept into our thinking. Even something as innocent as asking ministerial students to stand up in church suggests to students who are studying to be teachers, lawyers, and nurses that they are less Christian in their pursuits. Please don't misunderstand me. I don't mean to minimize the importance of the ministry. Rather, I mean to maximize that we are all called to minister. This subtle lack of unity, not seeing our lives as one piece of cloth, allows us to compartmentalize our work. As a result, most of us rush, push, or neglect some area of our work when we should be taking hold of our responsibilities in a calm and godly way.

I believe our lack of understanding of work has left a void within us that has allowed secular views of work to color our thinking. I see it not only among high-powered businesswomen but also among women earnestly employed in full-time Christian service. Consequently many of us are confused and suffer from a lack of direction and power.

Work Is Good

God created work before the Fall. In Genesis we read that Adam was to be co-laborer with God, to have dominion over the earth. Dominion is the God-given power to subdue the earth. Adam was to perform both mental and physical labor. He was to name the animals and tend the garden.

When Adam ordered and shaped his environment, he was imitating God. It was not a matter of what man was "supposed to do." It was a matter of his being God-like. *Work made man man.* Unfortunately, because of Adam's sin, work changed.

> Cursed is the ground for your sake; in toil you shall eat of it all the days of your life. Both thorns and thistles it shall bring forth for you, and you shall eat the herb of the field. In the sweat of your face you shall eat bread till you return to the ground, for out of it you were taken; for dust you are, and to dust you shall return. (Gen. 3:17–19)

In work we face the same dilemma as in the relationship between man and woman. That which was perfect is now blighted. Longings ordained by God go unfulfilled. Work, which was to stir in us feelings of accomplishment, creativity, and power (dominion) now also stirs in us feelings of failure, confusion, and impotence.

There's hope. As in the relationship between man and woman, work is redeemed by Christ. God gives us the ability to sift through the confusion and impotence of work. He restores our labor and makes it whole. Jesus Christ gives work meaning.

A Good View of Work

As creatures made in his image, we are to work the way God worked. We can imitate God in our labor in two ways. One way is by establishing order, helping to make something right. In the beginning there were form-lessness and darkness over the face of the deep. God's Spirit hovered over the waters and then he began his creative work. He said let there be light and sky and night and dry land and sea and seed-bearing plants and living creatures and people. And there were. God made order out of chaos. He worked, and it was good. He was tired and he rested (see Gen. 1–2:3).

We, too, can gain satisfaction from putting order where there is disorder, in restoring calm where there is none. It feels good to weed a garden, wash a car, clean out a closet, right a wrong.

We're happy because we've taken charge, established order, and used the abilities God has given us. We labor for the joy of creativity, not to prove that we're able, competent, or good at what we do. We're not looking for some payoff work might not provide. What we want is to use our mental and physical abilities to make this world a little more bearable. When we work as God works for the sheer joy of restoring order, we are no longer trying to *prove* something. We are demonstrating the reality of God. We are no longer trying to *find something*. We are simply, insofar as it is possible, reversing the effects of the Fall.

If we work this way we see more purpose in being a bookkeeper, a secretary, a lawyer, a teacher. Our work has new meaning. Each of us has the capacity to use our abilities to make this world a little more the way God intended it to be. We ask ourselves, is there any wrong here that needs to be righted? Is there anything I can do to fix this problem? Even if the wrong is only a messy file drawer, if we fix it, doing the best we can, we feel good.

Another way we can work as God works is by imitating Christ. God became flesh and dwelt among us, because he had work to do. Jesus said, "I must be about My Father's business" (Luke 2:49). He washed Peter's feet, wept over Jerusalem; he loved, he felt, he cried for others; he healed people and attended their celebrations. Yet whatever Jesus did, he did it as a servant doing his Father's will. Jesus was not trying to control those around him. He was not out to please the crowd, or to make new buddies. Jesus' work, quite simply, was to glorify the Father.

We can do that, too. We can help when it's least expected, give pride of place to someone who needs it, be pleasant so someone else's job is not quite so hard. In this type of work we ask, am I doing something to serve others here? Something that might give another person a little taste of joy? Am I in any way alleviating pain? Is another person better off because I'm doing this? When we work as Jesus worked, we find a deep satisfaction in our labor. We're not looking for someone to like us. We're not trying to prove ourselves to anyone. We're simply in the service of our Master.

When we stop designating "Christian" activities and "Christian" duties, we stop giving God that which already belongs to him and our work becomes whole. When we stop seeing one part of our lives as more valuable than other parts; when we stop seeing some people as more important than others; when we believe the work we do each day, whether it's scrubbing the bathroom floor, attending executive board meetings, or teaching Sunday school class, is what we are *called* to do, our lives change. Our emphasis shifts from an ego-centered push to "What next, Lord? What would you have me do now, Lord?" Our eyes focus on God. Gone are the labels and compartments from our lives. Goals and priorities change. We are free to be simply women who work. We are ordinary women leading ordinary lives in extraordinary ways.

Work As a Calling

Many of us resist the idea of work as a divine calling. If we think of Christ's becoming deeply involved in our jobs, we feel a little nervous. As I talk with Christians about their work, I notice this anxiety is not limited to "worldly" Christians (those whose thinking is obviously cultured by the world's standards). It is also true of Christians who appear to be trying with all their hearts to follow Christ and be obedient to him.

Anxiety at the thought of a divine calling occurs because deep down we fear we don't have what it takes to do the work God has called us to. We know that we *are* inadequate for our tasks and we're afraid we'll fail. That's not the bad part. The bad part is that when we realize our inadequacies the pain is too much for us to bear and we back away from our responsibilities rather than look to God as a model and guide. We avoid thinking about work as a calling at all.

Because we don't want to face our fears we figure out what we can cope with best and do that first. Then we miss what God has called us to do. We miss real living! We don't run the race totally abandoned, flat out, free. We don't trust Christ, and him alone, on a moment-by-moment basis. We run the race *very* carefully, trusting

God only every couple of days or every couple of years, and lead harried, fragmented, and undirected lives.

Unless we deeply believe in the power of Jesus Christ to sustain us on a moment–by–moment basis, we will never be able to act on our work as a calling. Many of us who look like pretty good Christians will miss the opportunity for real joy in the service of our Lord.

How can we change this?

By taking command of our thoughts and coming to grips with our worth to God. *Christ died for us.* God loved us enough to give his Son for us. *We must be important!* Taking ourselves seriously forces us to trust God. Elevating ourselves and the importance of our own lives to Christ also elevates him.

When we understand our own worth in Christ, we're forced beyond futile introspection to looking at the sufficiency of the Father. That's the key that unlocks our full potential.

The love of God gives us the courage to act *on* our surroundings instead of reacting *to* them. Instead of giving in to the pressures of co–workers, friends, family members, church groups, we ask new, simple questions: Lord, how may I serve? How may I love? What have you called me to do?

We see that he is the one who gives us the power to go into the office, the shop, the school, the factory; to suffer for doing good; to stand up for what is right; to eschew what is evil; and to love one another deeply. We see that it is impossible to separate God's work from our work, our work from his work, or our work from other areas of our lives. There really is a oneness to our lives in Christ, and the oneness gives us a deep inner strength.

We are *literally* made into new creatures. Elevating the importance of our lives in the light of the cross makes the difficulties of our work lose their hold on us. We view the long hours, the toil, the striving egos and harshness of co-workers and bosses in a new way. The pain and toil of work diminish in importance, and do you know what happens? Work becomes truly important for the right reasons. Despite the hassles and the problems, work becomes a way to express the wondrous image in which we're made, an opportunity to experience the joy of productivity, an opportunity to let love flow from us to others in the name of Jesus Christ. The love of God has overcome the world.

WOMEN IN PROCESS

*T*o flesh out the Christian concepts of work which we have been discussing, let's look at three types of women. The first woman is passive, paralyzed by her fears. She procrastinates and diverts her attention from the things that threaten her. The second, an aggressive woman, takes hold of her life, but because of her fear, she acts wrongly. The third woman, unlike the first two, is not controlled by her fears, but she does not always realize the joy that it is possible for her to have in the Lord.

Traveling the Road

To understand how these women live, picture the perfect will of God as a road. As the women walk along the road, they carry on their backs all the emotional baggage that's been piled on them over the years—anger, disappointment, insecurity.

Imagine that one side of the road represents the emotional response to withdraw, the other side the emotional response to attack. Both extremes are caused by fear. As each woman walks along, she has a tendency to wander off the road on one side or the other.

But imagine that up ahead of the women is Jesus Christ. They can see him standing in the distance calling out to them by name.

In the woods on either side of the road Satan darts in and out among the trees urging the women to withdraw or attack as the case may be. Sometimes Satan is out in the open, where the women can see him. But more often than not he conceals himself and his temptations and is hard to recognize. "Come," he says. "I'll help you not be afraid. Stop and rest a while in the cool woods. Don't worry about your journey. The woods are much more pleasant."

The Passive Approach

The first woman on the road has a tendency to withdraw in fear. She has learned over the years to avoid situations that might be painful. On her back amongst her baggage, she carries uncertainty about who she is as a woman. She's afraid that if she gives her job all she's got, she will somehow seem unfeminine. So she vacillates between being a "career woman" and being a "womanly woman." She's also afraid that if she devotes herself to her work, she'll somehow miss the opportunity for marriage.

She also carries anger. For openers, she doesn't even know if she *wants* to work and views her job as something that has been forced upon her. If she were married, she reasons, she might still have to work, but she wouldn't have to work so hard.

She also has doubts about her own potential. She's not sure if she's smart enough, clever enough, or talented enough to make a go of her job. Thus, she's also afraid of criticism. She feels that if she excelled in her work and committed herself to being faithful and obedient to God, others might resent or dislike her.

Because of the emotional baggage this woman carries, she tells herself she doesn't really care about work—it's not important. She doesn't feel her job is meaningful or that she's important in it, so she performs her work in a perfunctory way. Afraid to function with her whole being, she emotionally withdraws or procrastinates. She becomes passive. She allows her attention to be easily diverted by office gossip or problems with a co-worker. She spends much of her time lost in romantic fantasies or preoccupied with the fact that the Xerox machine makes bad copies.

Satan lures her off the road by telling her that work is too boring to be bothered with, her boss is too unappreciative, the position is beneath her, the pay is inadequate. He tells her to save her energy for the next job—or the perfect man. He tells her the important thing in life is her personal life—the one away from work. Or even her spiritual life—the one off the job.

Because she isn't motivated to do her best, she never experiences the deep satisfaction of hard work well done. She does not know what it is to grapple with Christian living at work.

The biggest problem holding us Christian single women back is passivity, which surfaces in avoidance—the refusal to quietly, in the name of Jesus Christ, exercise self-discipline, set goals, do something! Yet many times we don't recognize this reluctance as passivity. We spiritualize it or label it as being *balanced* or *submissive*. We consider it a Christian virtue and not what it is—a call from Satan to lure us off the road.

Our models, the godly women in Scripture, were not passive. They were strong. They were being all they absolutely could be. Esther risked death to speak to the king on behalf of her people. Ruth, a widow, accompanied her mother-in-law to a strange land. Mary, the mother of Jesus, after hearing the angel's astounding message replied, "Behold the maidservant of the Lord!" (Luke 1:38). The women knew who they were.

Avoidance and passivity are not submissive and balanced behaviors. They're wastes of time. And if we're Christians, time isn't ours to waste. It's God's time.

Whenever we don't use our best ability in our work, we're either ignorant of what a woman of God is supposed to be or are willfully disobedient. Once we know this and understand it, we have hope. Once we see how Satan fools us, we can expose him for who he is and continue along the road. Once we comprehend at a deep level the truth about work, we can resist the temptation to back off and avoid difficult work. We can look at our work as the opportunity for fulfillment as God intends it to be.

God wants us to know the courage of facing a problem and overcoming it—to know the wholeness that comes from accepting the challenge of work.

As we step out in obedience, we sense God's strength. We feel good and we want to become even stronger. Conversely, when we listen to Satan, no matter how trivial or unimportant his lies may seem, we fail to understand that daily living is holy.

Our callings are not something outside ourselves. They are projections of our created selves into an ungodly world. We do not simply react to our environment like an amoeba. We're capable of influencing our environment by being co-laborers with Christ.

Obtaining dominion over the space God has given us is possible. Our goal is to glorify him. Our identity is in Jesus Christ and not in the fearful person moving from one side of the road to the other.

We're not trapped as we often think we are. We're not locked into a meager existence so many of us settle for. The secret of success is not the push-and-shove that the world suggests; rather, it's being ready for God to use us when he calls.

God has called us to himself and to a purpose in our work. Can you imagine any reason why God might have you in the job you're in right now? Even if you plan on leaving next week, is there something you can do today to serve him? What can you learn about serving God in this job that you will use next year?

Begin with little things; start where you are, making small decisions quickly and positively. Fred Smith, in his book *You and Your Network,* observes, "Scraps of wasted time are where the winning edge is."[1] Wisely utilizing portions of empty time glorifies God.

We may have to do menial tasks for the rest of our lives, but menial tasks need not be unimportant. Although not everything we do is creative, much of what we do can be. It's possible to find new and increasing opportunities to be creatively involved in God's universe.

What new task would you like to do at work—one that doesn't require anyone's help or anyone's permission—one that would not take you away from your other responsibilities? Do it. What little thing have you been putting off that you could do right now which would make someone you work with happy? Do it. Is there something that you've been doing for a long time that you could, by thinking creatively, do more efficiently? Do it.

Striking Out

The next woman walking along the road responds in just the opposite way. She takes hold of her life all right, but she takes hold in her own strength. Many times she looks successful, but inside she's empty and afraid.

She may believe she can't depend on anyone but herself. Her experiences have taught her that people will eventually let her down, so she fears others' betrayal. She also believes that unless she *proves* she is worthwhile, she will not be worthy of others' affection. She's often angry at having to do certain work but believes that "being someone" is necessary and worth the cost. She wants everything now because she has little faith in herself or anyone else to sustain her over the long haul.

So she pushes her way to her goals by trying to win friends and influence people. She believes that advancing in her career and making more money will bring her happiness. She may be anxious to get more education or learn a new skill to solve her problems. She may look for a mentor, use the network, get in line to move up the ladder.

Although likable, cheerful, and fun to be with, she experiences underlying stress and anxiety. Her emphasis on performance causes her to manipulate others. She aggressively puts herself forward and occasionally puts others down. If this woman does not reach her goal, she becomes despondent until she finds a new one.

The world outwardly applauds her and the church distrusts her. The disparity between these two reactions draws her attention from the real issue, which is that she is called by God to do her best at work and appropriately fill her space in the universe.

A woman's work is not a weapon to use to defend herself against her worst fears, nor is it something to "be above." Work is good in and of itself. Work is admittedly painful because of God's pronouncement that it would be difficult. But Satan has greatly increased the pain of work by his blatant lies. His lie that we're only important if we're "successful" undercuts the essence of who we are. His lies about success make us feel guilty because we either long for what the world has to offer or feel cheated because we don't get it.

You may be saying with relief, "Well, I certainly don't fall for that. I know better than to feed on the world's success standards." Though we may not be fooled by Satan's more blatant lies, many times we fall for some of his more subtle tricks.

As Christian women, we may know for sure that we're called to work in the world. We may want to be top-notch for Christ, but this can be a compulsion rather than a godly desire. We can substitute a "pop-Christian" standard for the world's and then feel pious about it. Our deep inner fear of being found inadequate replaces the deep abiding trust that comes in fulfilling our calling. We don't respond to our work creatively or look for ways to establish order and serve others. Instead we respond to our work as a place to "move up for Christ."

It doesn't make any difference what our calling is, if we're always trying to prove ourselves, we can't discover what God has called us to be.

Many women who desire to be good at their jobs come in contact with motivational seminars on how to stay "up" at work, tapes on managerial strategies, and "how to" success books. Many of these *do* help us to perform in a more professional way at work. We can benefit from them if we are careful. The problem is that often the world takes Christian principles, strips Christ from them, and commercializes them for its own purposes. We Christians are attracted to them, both because they work and because they are vaguely familiar. The danger is that when we see these ideas working effectively during the work week, we may believe that all of the world's way of thinking is effective. If we believe too much of this commercialization, we cease to be uniquely our own. We become dressed-up copies of the world's originals, rather than allow God to make us the originals that the world copies.

Jesus Christ stands in the road and calls, "Come unto me all you who are burdened and I will give you rest. I'm going to give you a new mind, a new way of thinking. You don't have to struggle, push, or be defensive. I will provide all that you need. Lean on *me*. Feel the strength of my protective arms. Learn how to relax. Know that I am in charge. Sense the softness of your heart as you submit to me. Learn from me."

Practice thinking about God. Think of his love. Feel it. Two or three times a day, take a minute to relax in the safety of the Lord's love. When you feel yourself becoming tense or aggressive in an ungodly way submit to God. Ask yourself, "Can I trust God?" Because of your mindset, you probably will have inner doubts. That's okay. Think of the last time you lost control, and he came through for you. Now, willingly ask him to take your temperament and your personality and use them.

Ms. Average

The last woman on the road does not stray too far off in one direction or the other, but her pace is slow and she's often depressed.

She's conscientious and works hard all day long. After that, she grocery shops, does the laundry, and cleans the house. In addition to her vocation and her personal responsibilities, she also has an avocation. Her job is what she does to pay the rent, meet the bills, and survive in life, but at times it is not her first love. This is all right as long as she's meeting the spiritual challenge of work and is being conscientious about performing to the best of her ability the work that she is paid for.

What if her real love is her avocation? She may be a single mother whose primary calling is to her children or a woman with a beautiful voice who lives to glorify God on Sunday morning. She may be a woman who has decided to go back to school or a writer who knows someday she's going to write a novel with God as the central character. Whatever this woman's vocation or avocation, she knows she has to do them both.

Because she has an enormous number of responsibilities to juggle, she's often filled with self-doubt. She may be very close to having a divided mind. If she's not careful, she will respond to the "tyranny of the urgent" rather than see God's priorities on a moment-to-moment basis.

One of the pains she feels is her deep longing to have her avocation become her vocation. Desiring to work full-time at what she loves most is not wrong. God in his graciousness sometimes allows this to happen; sometimes he doesn't. A well-meaning friend may pierce this woman's heart by asking, "Don't you wish you could stay home with the kids?" "You're so talented, why don't you sing professionally?" "With all your gifts, why don't you start your own business?" Already overloaded, she becomes discouraged.

Questions like this add to her confusion and make her doubt the wisdom of God. It becomes difficult for her to see herself as called to anything—either her avocation or her job. If she isn't careful, she may misdirect her activities, go off in all directions, and then spiritualize her running around.

She's also very likely to have a problem with fatigue. She may believe she can handle more than she's actually capable of handling. Satan then attacks through the physical. Poor health habits such as eating on the run and missing exercise result in bad temper and depression.

Her biggest problem, however, is the temptation to believe she's never getting anywhere. Because there are so many demands upon her time, she gets discouraged easily. When this happens, she believes the reason she's not accomplishing more is that God doesn't love her or see her life as worthwhile. She fails to understand God's timing, God's purpose, God's will.

Jesus Christ stands ahead of her saying, "Don't take your eyes off me. You're doing a good job. I have given you all that it takes for you to do what I have called you to. You don't need to do anything more than be obedient to me. I will help you create order out of chaos."

Why do you think you exist? Sharpen that image. Define it. For what purpose do you exist right now—for this week, this year? Jesus says your priorities establish a lifestyle—they say who you are. He establishes your priorities based on whom he has called you to be. View each issue, each decision as an opportunity to go to God, to go before the throne to seek his guidance in all you do.

The Lord says, "I'm going to give you dignity of personality, the ability to make decisions calmly, and a sense of well-being and peace as you obediently go about what I have called you to. You will have a sense of mission and purpose as you establish your priorities, not with an eye on this life, but with an eye on eternity."

We all have a little of these three women in us. We all at different times passively resist our work, aggressively attack our work, or become burdened by our work and responsibilities. Once we recognize that Jesus is before us calling us to use our work to serve him, Satan's temptations become dimmer and dimmer, and we are able to respond to Christ's call.

FROM DISSATISFACTION TO DOMINION

O ne of the reasons we struggle so with work is that we blame on externals that which is our inner struggle—our striving to maintain both a passionate belief in God and confidence in our own self-worth.

Haven't you ever wondered, How do I get a passionate belief in God? How can I ever be like the saints and heroes of old? Can I ever gain the inner strength to be completely, uncautiously the Father's? On top of that, can I ever be genuinely confident in myself and my own self-worth? How can I maximize my potential—be all that God has called me to be?

We gain these goals by walking a hard road. We die to self so that we may live for Christ. We give up the defensive behavior that holds us back. We cast aside self-protective ploys so that we may gain the rewards of the Christian life—deep belief in God and abiding peace.

That's how we become not only hearers of the Word but also doers of the Word. We lay down our lives so that we may gain our lives and become women who can be used by God. This entails suffering.

The Last Mile

As I was reading through the first epistle of Peter, I found myself growing uncomfortable. The part that I love, "casting all your care upon him, for He cares for you," (5:7) did not make up for "Do not think it strange concerning the fiery trial which is to try you, as though some strange thing happened to you; but rejoice to the extent that you partake of Christ's sufferings" (4:12, 13).

My problem was I did not see myself as suffering for Christ. Even though I knew I was experiencing a profound personal relationship with God, I feared that maybe I was not in the will of God because I wasn't suffering. As I thought about this, I knew I had to confess to God the truth. I didn't want to suffer. I didn't want to go through any pain for Christ or anyone else, for that matter. I was afraid.

Then I realized that I do suffer in my pleasant middle-class life. I just didn't want to admit that what I go through is suffering. That seemed like defeat.

I wanted to deny the pain that exists in my life so I could avoid facing my own imperfections and the sorrow they bring. I wanted to drown out the disappointments of a fallen world by hoping against hope that my life, which may in fact not be too difficult, will somehow get better tomorrow. When I do this, I miss something that is very profound because the call to suffer is a call to healing.

Getting Satisfaction in Perspective

We're never going to be able to recognize our work as a calling without first recognizing that there is within each of us a craving for something we don't have. We understand that only God can satisfy us when we face the fact that everything we have ever desired—every job, every love, every possession, every event—has somehow disappointed us.

As we recognize what Pascal called the "God-shaped vacuum," and what C. S. Lewis referred to as a "longing for a far country," we recognize our own emptiness and we enter into the suffering of Christ. Rather than running away from the pain of life, we actively face up to the fall of humankind and we identify with Christ. Facing even the light pangs of suffering we experience each day frees our hearts and allows us to experience deeper emotions that exist within us. It allows more complex suffering to come out into the open.

For example, if I have a good job I look at it and say, "This really is a good job, but even a good job disappoints, and this hurts." It really *is* painful. Facing this light pain gives me the courage to long for something more. *It gives me the courage to long for God.*

Or, if I have a bad job, I say, "This really *is* a bad job. It hurts to have it. Life isn't fair." Then I turn to the Father, who has promised me fairness, justice, and reward in heaven if not sooner.

Satan doesn't want us to face up to the suffering we go through because if we do it directs us to God. Satan wants us to numb the pain. So we do. We put on manmade "armor" to protect ourselves from the pain of life. We arm ourselves against the inevitable struggle, but we do it in the wrong way.

Imagine again the three women walking along the road. These women have donned outfits of steel. In their effort to prevent their suffering, they have mistakenly tried to protect themselves with "armor" of ungodly behavior and they suffer even more.

Attempting to Protect Ourselves

The other day, as I was pulling off the expressway, I was confronted by a billboard picturing nothing but a name-brand whiskey bottle, twenty feet long, lying on its side. Over the bottle were the words, "After the work, the reward." Now I may not hit the bottle to vent my frustrations about work, but I may in fact eat a pint of ice cream late at night or go on a shopping spree that's not called for. When I do, I'm numbing the pain of work with an inappropriate reward, which is typical of the kind of armor we use to protect ourselves.

When we speed in traffic because our work has not gone well or skip work occasionally because our bosses make us mad, we're laying on defensive behavior through inappropriate rewards—or laying on armor to protect ourselves from the pain of life.

Another way we try to protect ourselves is by attempting to control our surroundings for the sake of convenience. We hide from the real issues in our lives by concentrating on things over which we have some control. We allow ourselves to believe if we could only readjust our schedules, find different jobs, or own the things we desire, we would be contented.

I am not a very orderly person, but still I feel so much the pain of inconvenience when paperclips are not in the right place, the tape dispenser is not on the desk, or my files are out of order. I become angry with myself or my associate. There's nothing wrong with my wishing I were more organized and working toward that goal. There is something wrong, however, with my numbing the pain of inconvenience with anger, with not acknowledging that no matter how hard I try, I can't always control my surroundings. When I become angry with myself or others over lack of that control, I am numbing the discomfort of inconvenience. I am pulling on armor to protect myself from the pain of life.

When a woman desires to control for convenience's sake she becomes very intent on rearranging her circumstances. She puts pressure on herself and others by becoming angry, tense, and manipulative. She fantasizes about what her life would be like if she *could* control her circumstances, and she says to herself, "My file cabinet drawer sticks. If I could just get that fixed . . ." or "If my pupils would just write their papers so I could read them . . ." or "If my boss would just learn how to use his intercom so I wouldn't have to get up and go in so often . . ." The list goes on. She is concentrating on the minor issues of her life as a way of avoiding more complex issues.

There's nothing wrong with desiring convenience and wanting our lives to run smoothly. But if we *live* at that level, we end up very shallow people. Yet that's what most of us do. We live at the level of our casual desires and hope for reward. We preoccupy ourselves and deny our deeper emotions.

We are consumed with convenience and reward because these are things over which we have some control. It is entirely possible that the file cabinet *will* be fixed or that the kids *will* write more clearly or that the boss *will* learn to use the intercom. All these things may indeed happen. So we think about them, talk about them, share stories with our friends. Then, as a treat, we end the day or the week with an inappropriate reward. That is how most of us live our lives, settling for inappropriate rewards and angry inside because we can't somehow get our lives settled.

Most people of this world experience deep, deep anger because, although they *may* get the file drawer fixed, it may be that they *can't* get their boss to use the intercom. Although they *may* get the kids to write neater, it may be that they *can't* find the Scotch tape when they need it. They *want* to control their lives and avoid pain, but they can't.

Moving Toward Satisfaction

What's the solution? Christ. Laying our lives at the foot of the cross, giving up all hope of convenience or earthly reward. In short, giving up all our casual desires and allowing God to make us new creatures.

How do we do this?

First, we look at ourselves for what we really are: willful. We realize that no matter how good we may appear as Christians, some part of us is still rebellious. One of Satan's tricks is to take the good in us and use it to deceive us, to prevent us from seeing our willfulness.

Second, after examining our habits and our lives clearly and rationally, we face our deepest fear, which is that the God who loves us is not really going to give us what we want. We confess to Christ that no matter how much we say we love him, deep in our hearts we fear. We become like the man who said to Jesus, "I believe; help my unbelief!" (Mark 9:24).

Third, we recognize that we have built walls around our hearts and say, "God, I am willing to suffer and break down those walls of fear that surround my heart. One 'stone,' one obstacle at a time, I will carry to the cross and give you."

The only way we will ever be able to do this is if we understand suffering, not as something to be avoided but as an opportunity in our everyday lives to identify with Christ.

Our women on the road, having prayed such a prayer, would begin to take off their defensive armor. They would take off their gauntlets of insecurity and shoes of pride, their leggings of anger and their armplates of willfulness. By giving up inappropriate rewards and all control for convenience, they would be moving more lightly along the road. All that remained of their armor would be the heavy steel plate covering their torsos—the armor protecting their hearts. By standing firm and waiting on God, they would begin to experience the reality of these words in the first epistle of Peter:

> But may the God of all grace, who called us to His eternal glory by Christ Jesus, after you have suffered a while, perfect, establish, strengthen, and settle you." (5:10)

The Final Stretch

When we stand firm and do not give up, no matter what, we are able to move to the level of hope.

Most of us have a deep hope for something. What we hope for is usually closer to our hearts than anything else. It is more important than mere convenience or reward. For most women, married or single, our hope is for love relationships that will satisfy. Common hopes about our work are: I hope I can find a job that will give me an opportunity to use my capabilities. I hope I can move up in my career so I can be better satisfied at work. I hope my boss will notice what I do, so I can get a promotion. I hope I can find a job closer to home, so I can spend more time with my children.

At the level of desire for convenience and reward, it is possible to have some control. *But at the level of hope, there is no control—only hope.* Maybe I *will* find a man to love me. Maybe I *will* get that job. Maybe my career *will* be advanced. Maybe my boss *will* notice me and appreciate me. Maybe I *will* get a job closer to home or making more money. I'll pray about it.

Hope motivates. It keeps us enthusiastic about life. Some women are able to sustain and live at this level of life. But most men and women are afraid to live at the level of hope because if a hope goes unfulfilled, the pain is too great to bear. To hope for something they may not receive, something they can't control, is excruciating. So many hope deeply for one or two things in life and then slip back into the dull, empty blindness of casual desires.

Certainly living at the level of worldly hope is better than having no hope at all. But worldly hope gives way to despair. The few who are able to live at the level of worldly hope move from one thing to another, achieving some of what they hope for and then hoping the next thing they achieve will better satisfy. When it doesn't, depression sets in. They become the walking wounded, empty because they have no hope.

The despairing need the hope of the cross. If we can dare to have worldly hope, and then willingly give up whatever it is we long for in life because of a higher hope, we can learn what it is to be godly women—to die to self.

We find that as important as we are to our Lord and although he gave his son to die on the cross to save us from our sins, we are nothing without him. There is indeed a discrepancy between what we desire and what we are able to achieve by ourselves. We understand that unless the Lord works with us, we can do nothing.

> Unless the LORD builds the house, they labor in vain who build it. Unless the LORD guards the city, the watchman stays awake in vain. It is vain for you to rise up early, to sit up late, to eat the bread of sorrows; for so He gives His beloved sleep. (Ps. 127:1–2)

After laying our inappropriate rewards and our desires for convenience at the foot of the cross, we are able to take off the heavy armor protecting our hearts; we are able to give up all hope of anything we have ever longed for, all hope for a husband, all hope for love, all hope for a career, all hope for financial security, all hope for dignity, all hope for ever being treated fairly, all hope of not being sexually harrassed, all hope for ever being really understood by others. When we dare to feel deeply those desires yet give them up anyway, we then suffer as Christ suffered—willingly!

With the three women on the road, we take the steel breastplates from over our hearts and allow ourselves to be vulnerable to the world. We stand at the place where one in one thousand dares to go because the risk is too high and the pain too intense. On the road, we meet Jesus who meets us where we are and covers us with the armor of God.

The Real Reward

Dying to self is not a mystical, biblical term we cannot experience. It's *possible* for us to give up always having to be in charge, having to be understood. We can eschew overeating, overdrinking, or sex as a way of reward. We can give up office gossip, pettiness, and jealousy as defenses. We can even give up hope of being someone "important" or "successful." We can give up aspiring for money, looks, and brains. We can accept ourselves the way we are as women of value to God, whom he will make strong.

According to my pastor, Steve Brown, Christians are called to die to self. They're not called to be wimps! We lay down our lives at the foot of the cross but we rise up strong! We are given new dominion—the God-given power to overcome the world. The place we work each day, whether it's office, school, church, or home, is where we take our stand.

Christianity is not ethereal jibberish isolated to one section of our lives. It's a driving force that permeates our souls. This driving force—the spirit of God working within us—*changes* our view of work. We have a godly confidence in our own abilities. We believe that each of us is individually useful to God.

We have God and his power, and the more we use his power, the more we sense not only the uniqueness of ourselves but also the fullness of God. Realizing this combination allows us to take the emphasis off the difficulties of work and put it on what God has called us to do. We are able for the first time to see ourselves in a new light.

We recognize our own worth and God's might, and it's no longer possible for us to blame those around us or our circumstances for our lives. We no longer feel impotent, angry, trapped by work. We have a godly strength. We are free! Work hasn't changed, but our attitude toward it has.

Living for Christ means that we strive with all our hearts to be what God has called us to be, but at the same time we taste an excitement in juggling work, play, family, and friends. Once we begin to experience the feel of it, it's exhilarating! We can almost sense if we go off course and seek to right ourselves again. We push ourselves. We train like athletes. Yet we know nothing can be done apart from God, so we lean all the more heavily on him.

Do you not know that those who run in a race all run, but one receives the prize? Run in such a way that you may obtain it. And everyone who competes for the prize is temperate in all things. Now they do it to obtain a perishable crown, but we for an imperishable crown. (1 Cor. 9:24–25)

We tap into the strength of Christ within us. Little stress is involved because we die to self and rise up more alive than we have ever been before. Christ makes a difference in our work world. We serve a *risen* Savior.

FROM DOMINION TO GLORY

Christ has called us to go out into the world and make a difference. He once commissioned twelve ordinary men who changed the world. We ordinary women can do no less than make a difference in our jobs.

Achievement and Acclaim

I think it would be wonderful if you became top producer on your sales force, speediest typist in your office, board chairman of your company, artist of the year, or winner of a Pulitzer Prize. Think of the satisfaction and acclaim if you discovered a cure for cancer!

Achievement feels good. Using our skills to the utmost gives us a tremendous high.

Often we receive acclaim for our achievements. Sometimes we don't. Although they should, achievement and acclaim do not always go hand in hand. This is disappointing. If we can learn to separate the two, we're better off. Working toward achievement and letting acclaim fall where it may takes the pressure off. That doesn't mean we should be mousy drudges or silent sufferers. It means letting God control our attitudes at work and not depending on other people's recognition of us.

In some jobs a high profile is necessary if we're going to remain upwardly mobile. Letting others know what we're capable of is quite all right. The key in putting ourselves forward is making sure we do so with honesty and integrity and without putting other people down. Once we reach the top, let's be kind. It's a great position to enjoy.

But what if we don't make it to the top? Sometimes we work hard and don't move up the ladder one inch. No one recognizes our godly effort. Jesus speaks specifically to this issue. He says those who would be first will be last. Those who are last will be first (Mark 10:31). It is those at the top who have to worry. Position, power, and success are heavy burdens to carry in a godly way. Our task is to keep from getting discouraged. It's extremely hard not to feel slighted or even angry when no one recognizes our worth. Working as God works and responding to our work as a calling helps us feel good about *what* we're doing.

Recently, a friend of mind shared with me that she envisioned a conference for thousands and thousands of single women who would hear testimonies by women who were excellent performers in their fields. She pictured presidents of large corporations, women in political office, inventors, scientists, owners of small businesses testifying that their successes were due to God's presence in their lives. I said I thought that was great, but I would also like to hear a secretary tell how she turned around the atmosphere of her company by working in a godly way. Another woman might tell how she had the courage to quit her job and move on to a better one because of her knowledge of God's love. I would also like to hear a single mother explain how, with wisdom from the Lord, she raised two children on a teacher's aid salary.

There will probably never be a conference like that. But when I go through the day making "good choices," doing tough but ordinary things which no one else knows about, I picture God in heaven applauding. I like to think of the angels getting excited and of there being joy all around.

Ethics

Most of us work because we need the money. There's no way around it. Most of us have to work to live. But where and how we work affects the quality of our lives. It would be cruel and wrong to say that if she just "trusts Jesus," the woman who has a miserable job will suddenly learn to love it. There are some jobs we will never love because they are intrinsically unlovable.

Many jobs are insensitive to human need. The pay is oppressively low, and bosses push unreasonably because of the pressure they're under themselves. Other jobs substitute management theory for real concern for the individual, and a woman may feel manipulated.

Some jobs exploit the weaknesses of others. A woman may not feel good serving alcohol to the local lushes every night or selling a product she doesn't believe in or even selling a product she believes in to people who don't want it.

Jobs in service organizations may be difficult because the needs far surpass our energy. Lack of time and resources in the job may cause us to feel we're only half serving the individuals we're being paid to help.

These issues and many more like them are matters of ethics. I don't know of a job that doesn't put us in a position of having to struggle to maintain a Christian ethic at work.

Many of us don't love our jobs because much of our work is subtly contrary to God's will. Ours is a fallen world, and whether we're Christians or not, that makes us uncomfortable at work. We can't make right the fallenness of man, but we can clarify the issues. We can commit ourselves to God's truths.

Christ calls us to open up our eyes and to see, to look at the world around us and to use our minds, to think about what's going on and not be afraid. When we do this we feel good. We face our jobs confrontationally and use the ability God has given us to reason, to think, to sift through the thorny issues of work.

I have never known anyone who dared to wrestle with ethical issues at work for whom God did not supply something they *could* do about them. Our willingness to meet ethical questions head-on helps stem the tide of oppressive frustration and anger. Confronting some of the very real and difficult problems of the workplace allows God to use us.

Christians have been on the cutting edge of work ever since Christ died. The reformers gave such a fresh meaning to the word *work* that today even the world admires the Protestant work ethic.

In the nineteenth century Christians rose up against the sweatshops, child labor, and slavery. Christian women were among the first feminists in the late 1800s. Today Christian women are involved in industry, commerce, government, medicine, education, and the arts. We touch the world. Establishing a Christian ethic at work may be the most important thing we do as Christians.

Using Our Gifts

God has given each of us various talents, gifts, or abilities which he wants us to use as part of our calling. Using the abilities God has given us inspires confidence in us, and it gives zest to our jobs.

Yet sometimes rather than utilizing our talents, work crushes them in the mechanics of efficiency. This hurts! Sometimes however, we ourselves ignore our talents. Because of low self-esteem, we don't believe we have anything to offer. We deny what God has given us. Or we may know we have gifts but don't have courage to use them. Perhaps we used them once and were rejected and are afraid of using them again. This rejection also crushes our sense of self.

Some women work in jobs where there is a no pairing of their responsibilities and their talents. It is possible for a woman to have a good job and lots of talent and still not have a job that uses her abilities. The saddest situation, however, is when a woman exercises her gifts and they're not appreciated. She uses them and no one cares.

Expressing our gifts at work is one way we answer our calling. Our gifts are part of our uniqueness, an expression of God in us. Using our gifts at work is what makes us feel our job deeply. If we don't express our talents in some small way, we become robots detached from our labor. This affects our relationships with those around us because we have no real connection with them as an expression of who we are. It also affects our relationships with God because we're not utilizing what he has given us.

Yet if we depend solely on the "right" opportunity and others' approval to exercise our gifts, we may end up incredibly frustrated. We cannot depend on other people to appreciate our abilities. Management and industry are of necessity self-interested. What we can do, however, is depend on God's approval and be willing to do our best each day. We can use our gifts in whatever small way that is appropriate and appreciate our gifts ourselves. This brings satisfaction to even the worst of jobs.

Let me be very tender here. I know many of you have good jobs, ones that don't hold you back. That's great. I'm happy for you. But some women have bad jobs, ones that don't utilize their gifts, or at least jobs that don't utilize as many of their gifts as they would like. If you're a woman who has a bad job, cry out to God, ask him for wisdom and help.

Wrestling with the world of work in an attempt to express ourselves creatively can be a tremendous growing experience. We don't want to fall into the inevitable emptiness that comes with moving from job to job and never creating something within the job we have. Making our way through the labyrinth of work, finding a balance between a job's demand and our own needs, takes skill, dependence on God, and confidence in ourselves. By not holding back, by attempting to use the abilities God has given us, we receive deep satisfaction and glorify the Father.

In a real sense a woman who is able to overcome a bad job has overcome the world.

Twelve years ago my sister-in-law found herself divorced and with two children to support. Having only a high school education, she took the best job she could find as a legal secretary. This job was bad only because it did not meet her financial need to plan for her children's college educations. Using what she learned at her job and her ability to understand creative financing, she turned her gifts into financial security. She now owns sixteen houses which she rents for income purposes! Her first child is through college, and she feels good.

Several years ago an artist friend of mine was out of work. I gave her a job running errands, doing things I didn't have time to do. Grocery shopping was on her list. When I returned home that evening, I opened my refrigerator and found a treat. Gone was the black, soggy lettuce. Wiped clean were the catsup and mayonnaise jars. Beautiful fruits and vegetables were artistically arranged in large bowls. She had used her God-given gifts of servanthood to please me and her God-given artistic talent to please herself. By cleaning out the refrigerator, she had taken some of the load off me. I loved her for it! By arranging the fruit creatively, she had done something for herself in a mundane job. Today she produces monumental works of art and is rarely unemployed.

Submitting to Employers

Much of management today is benevolent. It's in management's best interest to keep us happy at work. But sooner or later that inevitable conflict of interest on the job surfaces and a rebellious spirit rises up within us. We want what we want no matter what anyone says. As difficult as it is for us to handle, we need to take a stand for Christ at work with an attitude of servanthood toward our employers.

> Therefore submit yourselves to every ordinance of man for the Lord's sake, whether to the king as supreme, or to governors, as to those who are sent by him for the punishment of evildoers and for the praise of those who

do good. For this is the will of God, that by doing good you may put to silence the ignorance of foolish men—as free, yet not using your liberty as a cloak for vice, but as servants of God. Honor all people. Love the brotherhood. Fear God. Honor the king.

Servants, be submissive to your masters with all fear, not only to the good and gentle, but also to the harsh. For this is commendable, if because of conscience toward God one endures grief, suffering wrongly. (1 Pet. 2:13–19)

Any woman who has ever tried seriously to submit to an unreasonable boss knows how difficult it can be. Genuine submission is not easy and it can be complex. But we submit because we want to be happy; we want to work as God worked. In obedience to God we submit to our bosses.

Therefore I exhort first of all that supplications, prayers, intercessions, and giving of thanks be made for all men, for kings and all who are in authority, that we may lead a quiet and peaceable life in all godliness and reverence. For this is good and acceptable in the sight of God our Saviour, who desires all men to be saved and to come to the knowledge of the truth. (1 Tim. 2:1–4)

Our bosses may never change, but prayer changes our view of them. Through prayer we see them in a new way, as people whom God values, even as he values us. The main ingredient in submission is not acquiescence, but love. Prayer gives us the discernment and the power to love our bosses in a genuine way. Did you see the reward in Timothy's exhortation? God promises that if we pray for our bosses, we will be at peace, no matter how difficult our bosses may be.

True submission is a difficult quality to discern. It's an attitude of the heart. Many women who look submissive are really passive. Passivity is not submissiveness. There are women who are wrongfully passive at work, allowing their employers to underpay them and/or be insensitive to their working conditions. This isn't submission; it's a lack of self-esteem.

Some women look submissive because they don't have the courage of their convictions. They go along with anyone who has a stronger personality than they have. This isn't submission; it's the exploitation of their employers. Their bosses need their input in whatever way is appropriate and godly.

Passivity also has a flip side. Many women are passively aggressive—passive in their refusal to take hold of their lives, but aggressive in their responses. Rather than being angry at themselves for their own passive behavior, they become angry with their bosses, making them out to be the villains of their lives.

Some women may decline to take hold of their lives and come to view their bosses as their protectors, expecting them to stand up for them. When they don't, these women become quietly angry, feel cheated, and see themselves as victims.

Godly submission arises out of our fullness as women. Submission means to be all we can be as women created by God and yet to choose to restrain our desires out of respect and love for another. Submitting is hard, yet it is the way in which the world can most easily see Christ in us. Seeing a woman who is not neurotically passive but is strong and willing to submit because of obedience to an authority higher than mortals, simply confounds the world. They don't understand what they see, but they're deeply moved by it.

We don't always submit to our bosses—not when they ask us to do what is immoral or illegal. If this happens to you, make sure you have assessed the situation accurately.

Then seek advice from your pastor and an elder, as well as from a righteous woman. With a godly consensus and prayerful support, confront your boss. While letting him know that you respect him as a person, tell him in a reasonable way that you cannot do something that is against God's will. After that, drop the subject. He probably will either fire you, ship you to another department, or respect you and be glad you're working for him. In any event, you will have been a servant of a higher authority.

Co-workers

Do you remember in grade school how teachers described the marketplace as being the center of community activity? My teacher told us of oriental bazaars in the Middle East, farmers' markets in rural America, and trading posts of the old west. In each instance, the marketplace was a bustling place where people met, exchanged news, bartered with healthy competition, made friends, and banded together for trade. It was a good and exciting place to be.

I don't think the marketplace has changed much. Work is still a good place to be and for most people is the center of their weekly activities. But unless we have a godly overview of work, the competition, the conflict of wills, the pressure of schedules can eat us alive. Like atoms in a molecule, we and the people we work with ricochet off each other. Yet in this constant contact God uses us to touch the world.

There is an old saying that our lives are the only Bible some people will ever read. If we can use that idea properly—can avoid viewing work as a fishing hole or a place to gain scalps for Christ—and we can understand that it's not our job to manipulate or pull people into the kingdom, then the saying is a good one. The marketplace becomes a place to work as God works. We use our abilities and do the best we can because we want to experience the goodness of honest labor. We aren't out to prove ourselves because we know who we are. If there are those who feel they need to prove themselves to us, we understand and give up pride of place to them in love. We become their servants.

What about those times when we are genuinely mistreated at work? When others are unkind or our work is thwarted? We, like Jesus, weep over Jerusalem, the fallenness of man, but we love our co-workers anyway. We remain sensitive to their needs until God moves us on to another place.

I know this sounds pat on paper, but that kind of love, in a world which is hungry for love, is irresistible. If we continue to love our co-workers, even though we may frequently fail, they will be drawn to us. Holiness which is godliness in the true sense will show itself at work. Then even a job with difficult co-workers will have meaning.

Taking Charge of Our Money

God told us not to love or worship money. He didn't tell us not to earn it.

Poverty among women is a reality. The plight of elderly women, especially, has become a major area of social concern. Although much progress has been made in the last few years, in general, women still make less than men in comparable jobs. Because money is often identified with human worth, that hurts. It's also frightening. Money represents protection against hard times.

Fear, not low pay, holds most of us back. Because our basic nature is not to take charge of our lives and because most businesses exist to make profits, we women are often trapped by the very thing that makes us women— our nurturing, caring natures. Releasing us to the marketplace with our soft, gentle vulnerability, is like throwing lambs to a pack of wolves.

Our help with this problem is remembering that God has called us to be wise women. Being wise gives us personal responsibility and some defense against injustice. Once we have genuinely done the best we can, God takes over. He has promised to deal with those who oppress the helpless (James 5:1–9; Isa. 58; Pss. 10:17–18, 12:5, 140:12, 112:4–10).

When an employer or a company oppresses an employee, they're wrong and God's judgment is upon them. If we are employers, we need to understand this. If we are employees, however, viewing work as a calling helps. We take hold of our work before God, and our fear of money subsides. We work for God and use everything within us to do our best. If the company profits, there is no reason not to ask for a raise. We no longer see money as a means of security, which can be withheld from us, but as payment for work well done. This is because we are taking hold of our work in a way that God approves and for which our employers are supposed to pay us.

Sometimes they don't! So we have to be discerning. If your employers are misusing you and your co-workers out of a desire for unreasonable profit, they should be told this in a firm but kind way. Your attitude is really important here; militance is not the answer. At the same time you talk to your boss, however, it might be wise for you to look for another job. If you are the *only* one at work who is being "taken advantage of," you may want to ask why and examine the situation. Maybe you will learn something valuable about yourself—something that needs to change.

Sometimes a company can't pay you what you're worth. If you're doing a good job and have checked around and found the pay is not comparable to the same position in another company, you should change jobs. Make very sure you're not staying where you are out of an ungodly fear or guilt or desire for inappropriate affirmation.

Many of us are afraid of the responsibility that money entails so we don't bother to work effectively for pay raises. Others of us are afraid of even possessing money because we don't believe we deserve it. Some of us are getting personal strokes and feeling comfortable in our jobs because the work is easy. Others of us are in our jobs because we feel "appreciated" by those around us or because we have a certain amount of power or control in our positions. These are not appropriate reasons for staying in jobs for low pay. These reasons are not the fault of our employers. If we ask God, he will help us see ourselves clearly in relationship to money and work.

A Proper Balance

In not placing our security and sense of importance in money, we Christian single women have an advantage over secular women. But we still need to be certain we're able to distinguish between God's truth and popular ideas about money.

For example, the feminist movement, in a backlash of fear, has encouraged us to think like men which sometimes creates an ungodly aggression within us. On the other hand, Christian books and sermons on money, usually written by men, tend to create an ungodly passivity within us. We're buffeted on both sides. Men have a different attitude toward money from ours. Their sins are simply different. We don't under any circumstances want to trade our sins for men's sins. We don't want to pursue money out of fear, thinking it's a means of self-importance and security. The acquisition of money for power and as a symbol of our own importance is wrong. The *love* of money is indeed the root of all evil. But we can't afford to be passive in regard to our finances either.

If we are to have dominion over God's world, the proper attitude toward money is to make *provision* for our lives and for our futures without being driven by fears about our own worth and doubts about God's ability to provide for us. We're single women, and it's our responsibility to take care of ourselves. We're not to be burdens on our brothers in our old age.

Let me suggest a simple plan that you can start today.

1. *Tithe.* Give God ten percent right off the top.

2. *Pay yourself second.* Determine a godly amount (not influenced by fear or foolishness) that you would feel comfortable with saving each week and put it in the bank *today*.

3. *Be consistent.* Even if you save only a small amount, consistency is the key. Putting that money in the bank each week will make you *feel* great.

4. *Don't touch it.* It's as simple as that—leave it to grow with interest to meet your financial needs.

Most women don't save because Satan fools them into believing that investing is too complicated. Small amounts are not enough and larger amounts are overpowering. Even if you are badly in debt, with the help of a counselor, you can work out a system in which you pay yourself as well as your creditors a little each month. Listed below is an example of how a small amount of money can grow in a few years. Notice the importance of starting young! If you're older, don't get discouraged. God will honor your faithfulness.

INDIVIDUAL RETIREMENT ACCOUNT
Growth at 8 Percent Per Year

25-year-old:	$10 per week or $520 per year until age 65	=	$134,709
25-year-old:	$2,000 per year (IRA maximum) until age 65	=	$518,113
35-year-old:	$10 per week or $520 Per year until age 65	=	$ 58,905
35-year-old:	$2,000 per year (IRA maximum) until age 65	=	$226,566
45-year-old:	$10 per week or $520 per year until age 65	=	$ 23,794
45-year-old:	$2,000 per year (IRA maximum) until age 65	=	$ 91,525

The woman who is able to understand the value of money and still be openhanded with the poor is a virtuous woman. We are to live wisely and pay what we owe. But what does it mean to live wisely? It means to live within our incomes. Living within our incomes means not being obsessed with things.

Things

We go shopping and come home depressed because we couldn't buy the things we wanted. Yet when we clean out our closets we're overwhelmed by the number of things we have but don't need.

Some advertisers lure us by saying their products will make our lives easier. Others tell us that possessing

123

certain things means we have attained power, wealth, prestige. Our culture plays on every emotion within us to perpetrate our desire for things by feeding on our insecurities, our need for love, and even our guilt.

Ownership is valid. God owns the cattle on a thousand hills. He owns the creatures of the sky and seas. He owns us; we belong to him.

I will not take a bull from your house nor goats out of your folds. For every beast of the forest is Mine, and the cattle on a thousand hills. I know all the birds of the mountains, and the wild beasts of the field are Mine. If I were hungry, I would not tell you; for the world is Mine, and all its fullness. (Ps. 50:9–12)

Enjoying what God in his graciousness has allowed us to possess is good. At the same time, we must stand up against the world's standard of acquiring things. It robs us of our peace. We become driven by our sinful desire for power and possessions.

Try to separate your needs from your desires. Try to learn other ways to reward yourself than making a purchase. Analyze why you buy a certain product with a designer label or eat in a certain restaurant. If the reason isn't valid, then think of creative ways to change your behavior.

Try becoming a connoisseur. Select one or two items you already own and allow these items to be your pleasure. Separate the idea of money from the idea of worth. Eating a ripe strawberry, picnicking in the park, taking a moment to watch the sunset, even over the city, can be a lot more rewarding than going to the mall and costs considerably less.

Because "things" are so closely associated with work and money, we often don't realize what they truly cost us. What we purchase today can deprive us of security and pleasure tomorrow. Our possessions cost us time because we have to work for the money to buy them. Maintaining things we already own costs us even more time and more money. Yet America is so obsessed with things it's hard to resist the herd instinct without feeling peculiar.

But we must stand alone in the crowd.

The fanfare surrounding our possessions can strip us of what is really important. An inappropriate preoccupation with things brings leanness to our souls. A fuller relationship with God brings us contentment with what we own.

> But godliness with contentment is great gain. For we brought nothing into this world, and it is certain we can carry nothing out. And having food and clothing, with these we shall be content. (1 Tim. 6:6–8)

By looking to God and not to our possessions for happiness and a feeling of worth, we have a peace that lasts even if we have nothing.

What Happens When We Fail?

It's eight o'clock at night, and I'm sitting in an office that looks like the victim of a terrorist attack. This afternoon I was a little less gentle with a carpet installer who had rearranged his hour of arrival at my client's house three times. I am still paying on accounts left over from my days of financial unrest.

What happens when we fail at work? We recognize the grace of our Lord and Savior. We pick ourselves up. We ask God for wisdom and guidance. We ask whomever else we may have wronged for forgiveness. We face our situations head-on and we straighten out our lives. We keep on keeping on.

I'm sure many of you have your work pretty much in order. Your jobs are going well, your lives exhibit many godly virtues, you feel on top of the world. That's great. I'm happy for you. Enjoy it. But some of you may be exhibiting ungodly behavior or facing situations you don't know how to cope with. Do you hedge a little ethically? Are you intellectually lazy? Are you gossipy or overbearing with co-workers? Do you waste your money on foolish things? Take heart. Christ can give you the courage to act in a godly way no matter what difficulties you may have.

I have felt the very real embarrassment of failure, but I also know what it's like to persevere, to feel victory, to overcome. You can experience that joy, too. Whatever difficulty you're facing today, you can deal with it to the glory of God and in such a way that you make a godly impact on your world.

When Jesus gave the Great Commission he sent the disciples unto Judea, and to Samaria, and to the uttermost parts of the world. We begin at work, not with an ideal situation, but with an ordinary job. We straighten out our lives by working as God worked. We establish order and we serve those around us. Then, a little bit at a time, the best we can, as fast as we can, we establish dominion so that we can move on to higher ground.

PART THREE

BEYOND SINGLENESS

Happy is he who has the God of Jacob for his help, whose hope is in the Lord his God. (Ps. 146:5)

COURAGE   CHAPTER **10**
FOR
OURSELVES

*D*o you know what I wish more than anything else? I wish each of us could envision her potential for God and move toward that vision with excitement and determination.

To see ourselves beyond a traditional role is extremely difficult. Numerous secular studies have been made in an attempt to discover what holds women back. Why, when various opportunities open up for women, do some step forward, but many more hesitate?

Real visions are difficult for most of us. The average woman is reluctant to picture herself heroically. Sometimes it's easier to see ourselves through other people's eyes.

I see you as sharp, articulate, hard-working. In the many hours I've spent with Christian single women, I have been impressed with your energy, intelligence, and drive. In addition, I've found you to be tenderhearted and receptive to ideas about the Lord. I believe you are very close to God's heart.

But no matter how much I believe in you, I can't do here what feminists and anti-feminists alike have been struggling with for the past century. I can't motivate you beyond your inner view of yourself.

But God can. He has the power to give vision. He can and is willing to give vision to any woman who wants it. But there's a catch. We must give up our old dreams and be willing to receive God's dreams.

Women with Vision

The names of four women with vision are recorded in the genealogy of Jesus at the beginning of the gospel of Matthew. Three of them, Tamar, Rahab, and Ruth, were single when they followed their vision. The fourth, Bathsheba, was married.

Tamar, after marrying the two elder sons of Judah and being twice widowed, was denied the third son by her father-in-law. Tamar then did something that was shocking. She dressed as a harlot and seduced her father-in-law in order to bear the child that had been denied her. We are never called to emulate her sin, but Judah said of her, "She has been more righteous than I, because I did not give her to Shelah my son" (Gen. 38:26). Tamar stood upon the protective rights God provided for women in her day. Her trust in a God of justice gave her courage.

Rahab, the harlot of Jericho, was also a woman of courage. When two spies from the Israelite army came to look over the land of Jericho, they sought refuge in her house atop the city wall. Their coming presented Rahab with an urgent choice: she could either send the spies away and be safe or she could hide them in her home.

Rahab said, "The LORD your God . . . is God in heaven above and on earth beneath" (Josh 2:11). She hid the spies, and when Jericho eventually fell, Rahab and her family were spared. Rahab had the guts to believe in something greater than personal safety.

Ruth was a Moabite widow who chose to leave her home and follow her mother-in-law to Bethlehem. Having no one to take care of them, the two women were destitute. So Ruth went to work gleaning in the fields for food. Her hard work was noticed by the people of Bethlehem and she was admired and respected for the love she showed her mother-in-law. This devotion attracted the attention of Boaz, whom she eventually married (Ruth 2:11–4:10). Ruth chose to change the direction of her life by turning to Jehovah. She knew what she wanted and she chose a new God, a new land, a new hope.

Bathsheba, usually known for her adulterous relationship with King David, was also a mother. Her first son, conceived in adultery, died. David's grief was profound. In it he spoke the often quoted funeral text, "I shall go to him, but he shall not return to me" (2 Sam. 12:23).

Of Bathsheba's four sons, the most famous was Solomon. Jewish tradition has it that the beautiful passage Proverbs 31:10–31 was written by Solomon in memory of his mother. She must have been a remarkable woman. Even after her youthful charms had faded, she was still close to David as he was dying. He made Solomon, their son, his successor.

Though Bathsheba's sin was great, her loyalty to her son was also great. She was a woman of courage.

These four women, the first guilty of incest, the second a harlot, the third a Gentile, and the fourth an adulteress, were unlikely candidates to be mentioned in

131

the genealogy of Jesus. But I believe they were listed to show that God uses real people. They were mentioned because of their faith and not their perfection. They overcame difficult situations because their belief in God surpassed their immediate circumstances. I don't know about you, but that gives me hope. No matter what our sins may be or have been, our lives can be used by God!

The hope that gives women this courage and vision is not limited to biblical women. They line the corridors of church history. One of these was Marcella of Rome (A.D. 325–410). Marcella, born to a noble family in imperial Rome, opened her palace as a center for studying Scripture. It was one of the most influential Bible centers of the age. Marcella and the wealthy women in her group decided to give up the luxury of their social class and use their money to give blankets to the poor, money and food to the bedridden, and burials for paupers. One member of Marcella's group, Fabiola, was inspired to found Rome's first hospital.

When Rome was destroyed in A.D. 410, Marcella's house was ravaged. As the invaders beat her to death, she rejoiced that her wealth had all been spent in the service of Christ and that her treasures were laid up in heaven where thieves could not break in and steal.[1]

Paula (A.D. 347–404), a wealthy widow with three children and a convert of Marcella's, met Jerome, the church father and translator of the Vulgate Bible, at Marcella's study. When he decided to go to Jerusalem, he asked her and her daughter to go along. They did, and Paula used her enormous wealth to found three convents which she headed, a monastery which Jerome oversaw, a church, and a hospice to shelter pilgrims, orphans, the sick, the poor, and the elderly.

Paula served as an inspiration and intellectual stimulus to Jerome. As a matter of fact, he dedicated several of his translations and commentaries to Paula and her daughter. It was in her convents that the practice of hand-copying the Scripture was fostered. Through this method God's Word was preserved for the next one thousand years until the invention of the printing press.[2]

Christian women throughout history have worked, not only to transcribe Scripture and take their part in spreading the gospel, but also to nurture and tend the poor, the needy, and the oppressed. Hannah Moore, a woman of gentle breeding but tough spirit wrote many religious tracts and books in her day. First friends with such noted Englishmen as Samuel Johnson, David Garrick, and Horace Walpole, she was later influenced by Wilberforce and the movement for evangelical social reform. She was the one to call this period of English history the "age of benevolence."

Isabella Graham and Joanna Bethune were instrumental in founding the American Sunday School Union in 1817. The purpose of the first Sunday schools was not simply religious education as it is today, but rather to teach poor children to read and write. They met on Sunday because poor children at that time worked during the week in the factories and sweatshops. Sunday school was considered a tremendous threat to employers because they employed so many children. These women had courage.[3]

Elizabeth Frye, wife and mother of eleven children, was instrumental in prison reform for the female prisoners of Newgate Prison. Katherine Booth, with her husband, co-founded the Salvation Army. They were conducting a mission with prostitutes in 1865 in southeast London when they decided to "forsake the respectable chapels and reach out to the urban masses with the Gospel."[4]

Today, we may be too close to see those women around us who have the same courage and vision. But certainly one stands out because of her heroic work among the dying in India. She is Mother Teresa, Nobel Prize winner, a woman recognized by the whole world for her courage. The list could—and does—go on!

One Woman's Bones

One day while discussing great women of courage, one woman protested that it was not possible for her to live up to the standards they set. "They're special," she said. "They have something I don't have!"

This woman saw no relationship between herself and the great women of faith because she did not fathom God's goodness and his ability to move in her life. She had limited vision. She knew her life was valuable, but she couldn't see beyond the world's view of her. Because of this she was half-living and missing the joy that is possible in Christ.

Yet I identify with this woman, and I suspect many of you may too.

She doesn't believe she's being willfully sinful. She thinks that spending an enormous amount of time and emotional energy looking for love is what God wants her to do. "Aren't we supposed to?" she asks. "Isn't it natural, normal, what every woman wants?" She takes a lot of pride in her career. "I can't picture myself doing anything else," she says, "I've worked so hard for this job and I use it to glorify God."

This woman wants what most of us want—to love and be loved, to have our life's work be fulfilling. These desires are not wrong unless we pursue them in a way that God has not designed for us. If we do, they become

134

"bones," something tough to lug around, something meant to be buried.

Giving Up Old Dreams

Steve Brown uses an illustration about Joseph, the son of Jacob who had the coat of many colors. Before Joseph was sold by his brothers into Egypt, Jacob bought a little plot of land in Canaan, in a place called Shechem. Years later, after the famine and after his father and brothers had settled in Egypt, just before he died Joseph made his family promise to carry his bones back to Shechem to his father's plot of land.

Three hundred fifty years passed from the time of Joseph's death to the Israelites' entrance into Canaan. The Jews went through years of captivity in Egypt, years of wandering in the desert, years of fighting their enemies, but still they carried those bones around.

It couldn't have been easy. But they did it.

And God was faithful.

God finally brought them back to Shechem. Can you imagine what exaltation there must have been the day they buried Joseph's bones? What excitement, what relief, they had made it home!

Many of us are carrying "bones" around waiting to take them someplace. Dreams that haven't come true, crushed hopes and unfulfilled longings, are like bones we need to bury. We're not taking hold of our lives because we're unable to imagine a God who loves us with an eye on eternity and an eye on this world as well.

Because of our limited views of our relationship with God, we sometimes feel isolated, misunderstood, and out of step. Even though we're often hopeful, we're hopeful for the wrong reasons. We're trusting God to provide the substance of our fantasies, rather than what he's actually promised to provide. We're looking for something readily identifiable rather than grabbing hold of real life as it unfolds.

With both our eyes on this world, we see life only in terms of traditional roles, whether wife and mother or career woman. We don't see God's ability to create new roles for us. Because of this, we lack godly hope and are sitting on the fence, afraid to risk his way.

Jumping off this fence isn't easy for any of us. It means letting go of old dreams and some future dreams, giving up what we've been told all our lives would satisfy us.

That's just plain scary. It took me years before I was willing to make that leap of faith.

But I did jump and it feels good.

A Solid Hope

The woman who jumps off the fence has hope, not in her own ability but in God's. She's a wise woman, choosing to live in undivided devotion to the Lord. Single-minded, she has put her hand to the plow and is not looking back. She says to the world, "Don't pity me because I'm single. I know who I am. God has not deserted me. He has created a unique space for me to fill. He has given me a life and I'm living that life to his glory."

What helped me decide to risk God's way was a conscious effort to change my thinking. I actively decided to believe that what God had to say was true—that no matter how unnatural it might feel or how much I might not like it, I would believe that it's not God's desire to restrict me, but that it is in my own best interest to live in undivided devotion to the Lord

Thinking this way doesn't come easily to most of us. It takes a conscious effort.

By God's grace, it's possible to have a deep belief in God's love and in our value to him. We can emulate the great women of godly hope by looking beyond immediate, earthly dreams to a heavenly city. We can develop a vision of who God has called us to be and prepare ourselves to be ready for the Master's use. Trust in God is never misplaced trust. He is waiting for us. There is a place for our dreams in Shechem.

A NEW MIND

A woman in our prayer group came to me one day. Frustrated, she blurted out, "What's wrong, Gigi? Why do I act like this when I know Christ loves me? Why do I do the things I do?"

This woman was not a "wayward wanderer." She was a Christian single woman experiencing inconsistency in her life, and it bothered her. I experience inconsistency in my life, and it bothers me too. So I ask myself: why? When we have a God who loves us, when we say that we want to live for Christ, why do we nice, sincere Christians do things which are so detrimental to our lives?

We have seen how backgrounds, fears, and prejudices can cause each of us to build up wrong ways of thinking which, although often subtle, cause us to act sinfully.

Wrong patterns of living are always based on wrong philosophies of life. We aren't godly women when we know we should be and we do the things we do when we know we shouldn't because we've been fooled by the

139

world. Living this way may work temporarily for some women, but for the Christian single woman who desires to be obedient, it's disastrous. It causes her to be confused, doubleminded, and spiritually impotent.

> And do not be conformed to this world, but be transformed by the renewing of your mind, that you may prove what is that good and acceptable and perfect will of God. (Rom. 12:2)

Transforming our lives involves changing the contents of our minds. We were all born with foolishness "bound up" in our hearts (Prov. 22:15). Daily our minds are exposed to false ideas about how to be happy and feel worthwhile. These false ideas pummel us from all sides. They make us desperately afraid. Fear binds us.

The Beginning of Courage

Great acts of faith are built on little acts of courage, but to have victory over even the small decisions in our lives we must first break the fear that binds us. Living our lives each day making small but difficult decisions for God is hard. No one else but God really knows the war that goes on within our souls. To become women of courage we start at home with small everyday decisions and build on those decisions until God moves us on to carry out his will in the world.

In their book, *Encouragement: The Key to Caring,* Larry Crabb and Dan Allender explain fear this way. Before the fall of man, "Adam enjoyed unclouded fellowship with God. There were no walls, no distance, no tension. But sin immediately brought terrible consequences. Among these was the presence of a new emotion: fear."[1]

When Adam and Eve disobeyed God's command, they were afraid and hid from God. Have you ever wondered why they bothered to hide from a God who is omnipresent—who knows everything anyway? Their actions are an example of what our fears do to us: they make us unreasonable. But God loves us, he reaches out, he doesn't leave us alone.

God called out to Adam. "Adam, where are you?" (Gen. 3:9). God knew where Adam was, but because he loved him he wanted to expose Adam's behavior. Explain Crabb and Allender, "Only exposed problems motivate people to ask for help."[2]

Adam replied, "I was afraid because I was naked; and I hid myself" (Gen. 3:10). At this point, Crabb and Allender break down Adam's response into three distinct parts:

1. I was afraid: Adam's core emotion;
2. Because I was naked: his core motivation;
3. So I hid myself: his core strategy.[3]

In one form or another, we all play out the same scenario in our lives. We are afraid because we are naked, so we hide. What goes on within us and in our world is genuinely threatening. We have reason to be afraid. So we hide ourselves behind a drink or two, a new dress, boasting or shyness, flirtation or efficiency. We hide to keep ourselves from exposure. Like Adam, we choose our own means of hiding, and we miss the solution God offers.

So that we can come out of hiding and stand up unafraid, so that we can change our old dreams and our wrong philosophies of life and become what God has called us to be, let's look at ourselves the way the authors of *Encouragement* looked at Adam. We are 1) emotional beings capable of feeling, 2) thinking and motivational beings able to reason, and 3) volitional strategic beings capable of making choices. We all have each of these capacities within us. Dr. Crabb, in his book *Effective Biblical Counseling,* further explains that these three capacities form a *whole* thinking, feeling, and volitional person.

A Model for Wholeness

What does it mean to be a whole person? Let's look at ourselves in a hypothetical way, dividing ourselves into three entities each represented by two circles. One entity is the ability to feel—our emotional circle; another is the ability to choose—our volitional circle; the third is our ability to think—our rational circle. Together these circles make up our personal wholeness. If we are whole persons, thinking, choosing, and feeling the way God intends, the inner circles (our actual experience) will fill the outer ones (our God-given capacity).

RATIONAL WHOLENESS + VOLITIONAL WHOLENESS + EMOTIONAL WHOLENESS = PERSONAL WHOLENESS

None of the inner circles in the illustration is complete. That's because none of us is perfect before reaching eternity. Much of the time we aren't thinking accurately, choosing correctly, or feeling fully. Our circles can become more complete only as we depend on Christ. Otherwise we respond like Mary, Janet, and Dawn.

Mary

Because of hurt in early childhood, Mary blocks her feelings (incomplete emotional circle). She is extremely self-disciplined (incomplete volitional circle). She thinks that achievement will make her secure (incomplete rational circle), and the race for security has left her exhausted and empty. Mary is looking to achievement rather than to Christ to make her whole. She is a Christian and she is successful, but she has no sense of her personal worth and acceptance in Christ. Because of this, she feels tense and anxious a great deal of the time. Her circles are not complete.

Janet

Janet does not feel anything deeply (incomplete emotional circle). She acts cautiously (incomplete volitional circle). She thinks it's better not to risk than to risk and lose. Because Janet believes she is the sole master of her fate but cannot always control the circumstances in her life, she is often depressed and indecisive (incomplete rational circle). Janet is looking to her own ability to control rather than to Christ to make her whole. Janet cannot always structure the outcome of her world, so she tries to make as few decisions as possible. Though she is a Christian, she would rather not reach out at all than reach out in faith.

Dawn

Dawn is an overly emotional woman (incomplete emotional circle). She acts on her moods (incomplete volitional circle). She thinks she has to see a manifestation of love in order to feel secure (incomplete rational circle). Because her friends can't always be relied upon to remember her birthday, call at the right time, compliment her on her dress, she is often disappointed. Dawn is looking to other people rather than to Christ to make her whole. Dawn's dependence on people causes her to be temperamental and unhappy much of the time. Although Dawn is a Christian, she is not experiencing the peace and joy God desires for her in her life.

Having incomplete circles does not mean these women don't at times experience satisfaction or joy in the Lord, but because of defensive behavior based on wrong thinking, they have *less* satisfaction than is possible for them to have in Christ.

Change Is Possible

We are all sinners affected by our sinful world. This causes us to act, think, and feel in sinful ways. But through the Holy Spirit, we can be changed with Christ! We can have lives guided by Christ instead of our defensive behavior.

God created us with the capacity for a relationship with him and for enjoying life with purpose. When Adam and Eve rebelled against God, these capacities became needs—searing needs that demanded satisfaction. What God once intended to be a fully met capacity became an emptiness, an unmet personal need.

Unmet needs result in a sense of personal emptiness which we usually try to satisfy in some way. It's good for us to understand ourselves and our needs and to teach ourselves at the point of our weaknesses to turn to Christ rather than inappropriate or ungodly behavior. Dr. Crabb identifies the two needs within us as the need for security and the need for significance.

Security: A convinced awareness of being uncondi-
tionally and totally loved without needing to change in
order to win love, loved by a love which is freely given,
which cannot be earned and therefore cannot be lost.

Significance: A realization of personal adequacy for a job
which is truly important, a job whose results will not
evaporate with time but will last through eternity, a job
which fundamentally involves having a meaningful impact on another person.[5]

These personal needs for security and significance can
only be met in our relationship with Jesus Christ. No
matter what our difficulties may be and no matter how
insolvable our trials may seem, if we look to Christ to
meet our needs for love and importance, he will give us
the capacity to grow in personal wholeness.

Rational Wholeness

God does not want robots or timid mice. He wants
women with the ability to think—and think correctly.
Before the Fall, humanity was able to reason. After the
Fall our thinking became futile and our hearts darkened
(Rom. 1:21). In other words, our *capacity* for thinking has
not changed since the Fall, but because of sin, the *accuracy*
of our thinking has.

Thinking Error #1: The solution to my personal
problems depends on a change in my circumstances.

"I would be happy (secure/significant) . . .

   . . . if I were married."

   . . . if I were more attractive."

   . . . if my parents hadn't rejected me."

   . . . if the church had a better singles group."

   . . . if I had a better job, more money, nicer clothes."

Believing a change in our circumstances would make us happy puts the emphasis on our circumstances instead of our relationship with God.

This does not mean that it's always wrong for us to change our circumstances, but when we allow ourselves to believe that the externals of our lives—careers, achievements, husbands, friends, finances—are the things that determine our fulfillment, we're simply wrong. This is Satan's lie. Our fulfillment and our joy are internal. They are our hearts' response to our commitment to the Lord.

Concentrating on things outside ourselves shifts the responsibility for our growth from our own actions to things and events. We believe we aren't responsible for change until our circumstances change. We believe we can't grow as Christians until life improves. We become trapped by what goes on around us: by people other than ourselves, by things other than ourselves, by situations we can't control. We become either highly controlling people or "victims of our circumstances."

"My job is so unfulfilling. I don't get along with my boss. I think I should change departments."

"If I were married, I wouldn't have to worry about inflation and how to pay the electric bills."

"If the sermons were better on Sunday morning, I would grow more as a Christian and be a lot happier."

Single women in our culture are subtly taught to depend on others for their fulfillment. It's difficult for us to see ourselves as being responsible for our own lives. Yet no one else can live our lives for us. When we fill our minds with the thoughts that career, husband, money, or *any* other set of circumstances is going to make us loved and important (secure/significant), we miss leaning on

Christ, who is the giver of all good gifts. We miss experiencing Christ as the lover of our souls.

Thinking Error #2: The solution to my personal problems depends on changing how I feel.

"I could do what's necessary if . . .

. . . I felt more secure."

. . . I didn't love him so much."

. . . I felt better about myself."

Women, more than men, are taught to experience their feelings. Feelings are very real; however, when feelings dominate our thinking, they take the place of action. They rob us of power.

"I don't *feel* like straightening the house. I think I'll watch TV."

"My boss makes me so nervous, I *can't* work properly."

"I gain weight because I *love* ice cream."

"I'm so *happy* today, I think I'll skip school."

"I *love* him so much, I'll do anything he asks."

Feelings are a beautiful and tender part of being a person. God wants us to experience our emotions. It's only when we think these feelings or emotions are more important than our obedience to God that we get into trouble. When our feelings and emotions control us, we miss trusting Christ as the Lord of our lives. True peace, joy, and contentment elude us.

A woman who reasons in a godly way is able to sift through the expectations of the world as conveyed by TV, movies, and peer pressure. She rejects any thinking contrary to her belief that Christ alone is the basis for her joy. She takes hold of her mind, evaluates events, and *consciously decides* how she will think about her circumstances. She makes her evaluation based on Scripture and by faith. She depends on her knowledge of Christ and not her emotions to guide her life.

Volitional Wholeness

God created women with the ability to choose, and with that ability came the responsibility for our choices. That's pretty frightening for me. I have trouble acting on what I know to be true. I like to skip through life, enjoying its pleasures. I don't like to think about the consequences of my choices. What a fool I am!

I'm free to overeat, but if I do, I'm not free to fit into a size ten dress.

I'm free to sleep late, but if I do, I'm not free to make my nine o'clock appointment.

I'm free to leave dirty dishes, but if I do, I'm not free to come home to a clean kitchen.

God gives us the freedom of choice, but not without consequences. We need to understand that we're responsible beings, responsible for our lives. Do you think it's possible to be nice when you're hurting, to say no when you love pizza, to read your Bible when you're mad? One of Satan's biggest lies is to make us think we have to *feel* like doing something before we do it. We can *choose* to behave according to God's will, whether we feel like doing it or not.

Carolyn had been dating Jim for three months. He stopped seeing her and started bringing Ann to the singles' fellowship. Carolyn felt resentment, anger, and jealousy toward Ann. Eventually, however, convicted by God's Word, Carolyn began to think (reason): "I feel jealous, but I can choose to act lovingly. I feel resentment, but I can choose to be nice." Carolyn set her will to do God's will. She *chose* to act biblically regardless of how she felt.

148

Terri felt trapped by lousy circumstances. Everything in her life was going wrong: poor health, money problems, family crises. Under enormous pressure, she began searching for an outlet in an attempt to find relief. She fantasized about the man in the next office and about spending sprees she could not afford. Encouraged by a friend, she began to change her thinking. She thought (reasoned): "I am tense, but I can choose to release that tension in a way acceptable to Christ. My health is poor, but I can trust God's merciful wisdom." Terri stood strong. Her circumstances didn't change, but her thinking did and sinful actions were averted.

To say *mechanically,* "I want to do this, but I choose to do something else," or "I feel like this, but I trust God for that," is not sufficient. When we blindly live life the way we are "supposed to" or the way we "should," we miss the point of obedience. Genuine results are brought about by believing God's truth. Are the propositions of Jesus Christ true? If they are, we can choose to act consistently with our belief in truth.

A good thing to remember is *we always do what we want to do.* We are volitional beings. We live by what we *think* will work for us. Carolyn and Terri were able to change their actions because they were *willing* to change what was going on in their minds.

When we say "I have to" rather than "I choose to," we feel controlled. We don't experience the freedom God intended. Lack of personal freedom creates interpersonal pressure. We may feel as if we *have to* do certain things because of the expectations of family or friends, acquaintances.

"I *have* to write my grandmother."

"I *have* to go to the Bible study."

"I *have* to invite Judy over for dinner."

A better phrase to use for "I have to" is the phrase "I choose to."

Remember, in any given situation we always have a choice. We may not like our choices, but they exist. Unfortunately, the consequences of some choices are obviously much more difficult than the consequences of other choices. As godly women, we are able to reason: what is responsible thinking? What would God have me to do in this situation?

"I choose to write my grandmother because she is lonely and would enjoy a letter."

"I choose to go to the Bible study because I want to learn more about God."

"I choose to invite Judy over for dinner because I want to develop our friendship."

As volitional beings we will sometimes choose not to perform according to other people's expectations.

"I choose not to write my grandmother because she's controlling me and I don't want to be manipulated."

"I choose not to go to the Bible study because I have overextended myself and I'm tired and I need the rest."

"I choose not to have Judy over for dinner because I want to do my laundry."

Do you see the freedom that comes from "choosing to" rather than "having to"? A lot has been written lately about women and assertiveness. Much of it is good. Our concern here, however, is not in becoming assertive, but in becoming obedient: choosing to think and act biblically.

As volitional beings, we think of our problems not as matters of emotion or circumstance, but as matters of will. We need never be forced by emotions, people, or situations to do anything. We can choose the direction of our wills.

Emotional Wholeness

Feelings, how they control us! Often whether we know it or not. About twenty years ago feelings became king in America. We were told to be true to our feelings, get in touch with them, let them all hang out. We were encouraged to share our emotions at a gut level with almost anyone who would listen. The implication was that holding back our feelings was certain to impair our mental health. Today there seems to be a shift in the other direction. Whatever the current trend, our feelings are real. A proper understanding of them is essential to our spiritual growth.

Let's begin with hidden or blocked emotions. We're all emotional beings whether we look like it or not. When we feel good, we're unstoppable, but when our feelings are painful we want to die. If they become unbearable, we block them out. We pretend they don't exist. Denying or blocking our feelings is like trying to sink a balloon. Pushed down in one place, they surface in another. Blocked feelings can result in irrational and even immoral behavior.

Ann loved Jim. Jim did not call Ann. On Saturday night, Ann went out with Scott and went to bed with him.

Penny's mother expressed concern over Penny's not being married. Penny went into her room and went to bed. She took two pieces of chocolate cake and a coke with her.

The week after Linda's rent was raised one hundred dollars, she worked sixty-three hours. In order to make sales, she lied to her customers.

When we block our feelings, we are, in fact, denying a part of ourselves. The proper way to handle difficult feelings is to acknowledge them. *Unexpressed* emotions don't cause problems; *unacknowledged emotions do.*

When Ann did not get a phone call from Jim, she may have shrugged her shoulders and thought, "What do I care about him? He's a jerk." But she did care. In fact, she was very upset. She had blocked her feelings of rejection. When she denied those feelings they created in her a tension she had to discharge. Because her emotions weren't under her *rational* control, she discharged her tension in reckless behavior, which was also immoral. Sex with Scott "worked" because it made her feel better. She had more choices about how to deal with her feelings of rejection, but she didn't see them because un-acknowledged feelings lead to a reduced awareness of choices.

When Penny's mother made the comment about her not being married, Penny winced inside. Her mother was implying, "I only value you as a woman if you're married. I only think of you the way I raised you—to have a family." Penny was hurt by her mother's subtle rejection, but she could not admit, even to herself, the anger she felt over her disapproval. She answered her mother nicely, "You're right, Mom. I sure hope I get married someday," and her unacknowledged emotion created in her a volcano of tension which she released by eating.

When Linda's rent was raised one hundred dollars, she panicked. She had no money in the bank, no husband, and she wasn't sure she could trust God. But, rather than acknowledge her fears, Linda said, "I can handle this. I'll figure out a way to work harder." As a result of her unacknowledged fear, Linda worked long hours. She didn't choose to honor God and act responsibly. Under different circumstances, working harder might have been a proper choice. But for Linda, it was a compulsion. Because her goal was to relieve her tension rather than ask God to help her find the answer to her problem, she allowed herself to compromise by lying.

Do you hide from your feelings from time to time? Do you avoid and block your emotions? Ask God to help you get in touch with how you honestly feel. Ask him for the confidence to face your fears. Ask the Holy Spirit to reveal the thinking that underlies your behavior. Search your heart. Test your emotions. Ask yourself: how am I feeling? What has happened to create that feeling? Then turn to Christ for revelation. No emotion is so sordid, painful, or frightening that God cannot deal with it. The more we know about his character, the less we will be afraid of our own.

Remember, you don't have to express your feelings to find relief from them. You do need, however, to acknowledge them. Unacknowledged feelings lead to a reduced awareness of choice.

A better way for Ann to act when Jim didn't call would have been for her to tell God her feelings. She might have said, "God, I feel hurt, angry, rejected." Once her feelings were recognized and acknowledged, they would have had less power to control her. Later, when she went out with Scott, she would have been more aware of her choices and realized she didn't want to go to bed with Scott. She would have been free to enjoy him simply as a friend, knowing it was enough that God knew the pain she felt about Jim.

On the other hand, Ann's feelings may have been more complicated. Her feelings of rejection may have triggered in her a new feeling—the feeling that she could not control her sexual behavior. Lust is seldom the only underlying emotion expressed in sexuality. A desire for acceptance, comfort, emotional control, or revenge may also have come into play. Ann may have had one or many of these emotions and wrongly believed they could be satisfied with sex. To maintain control over her emotions, Ann then needed to acknowledge these new feelings and wrong beliefs to God.

A better way for Penny to react would have been for her to express her feelings of rejection to God and ask him to show her how important she was to him whether married or single. Her mother was believing and acting out of a wrong view of life, but there was no reason for Penny's thinking to become theologically unsound. Had Penny acknowledged her feeling of rejection to God and confronted it, she would have been free to analyze her mother's wrong thinking logically. Then she might have chosen to remain silent about the matter, or she might have chosen to speak to her mother about a single woman's worth. In either case, she would have been making a choice based on her strength in Christ, and she would not have reacted defensively.

A better way for Linda to handle her rent increase would have been for her to acknowledge her feelings of fear and panic to God. She might have said, "God, I'm afraid, helpless, alone; what can I do?" She could have prayed for right thinking and a godly solution. After prayer, she might have decided to try other avenues to meet her need for the rent money—finding a roommate or a smaller apartment, for example. Having acknowledged her emotions and thought rationally, her actions would have more likely been based on biblical solutions.

Let's suppose Linda prayed for more sales and didn't get them. She would have again acknowledged her feeling of fear to God and, on top of this, a new feeling of disappointment. She then may have prayed for the willingness to wait for God and, at the same time, courage to look for other solutions to the financial crisis. This type of interaction with God brings about true peace, with less fear and tension.

To review, our feelings are the exterior surface of our inner core. They often block our proper thinking and our proper choices. *Unexpressed* feelings don't cause problems; *unacknowledged* feelings cause problems. The proper way to acknowledge our feelings is to express them to God. Then we can decide whether or not we want to express those feelings to others.

Completed Circles

We all want to be women of courage, but often we're women in rebellion against God. We're trying to make it on our own, to do our own thing, to go our own way. Luckily, we were created in such a way that this isn't possible. No matter how hard we try, we simply can't function effectively without Christ. Because of our efforts to live without Christ in the center of our lives, we created problems in ourselves. These problems won't go away until we're able to do that which takes the most courage of all—to complete our inner circles and become whole women of God.

A personally whole Christian woman will evidence certain characteristics:

• She will be willing to fail. She may be afraid of failure, she may not like it, but she'll keep on keeping on because of her personal conviction that Christ's way is true.

• When other people disagree with her, disappoint her, or disapprove of her, she'll be able to remain objective, open, and compassionate. Knowing that there is nothing that can shake her worth in Christ, she'll not be insecure.

155

• She'll be open to looking at her own faults. She'll be able to accept criticism, analyze her problems, and profit from the opinions of others.

• In the middle of a crisis (lost love, lost job, death of a loved one) she'll remain steadfast in her determination to live for the Lord. Although she may experience intense emotional pain, she'll resolutely declare, "I will follow Christ, no matter what."

• Most important of all, she will be willing to serve Christ even if encouragement does not come and all her efforts seem futile.[6]

To become women of courage, we examine our emotions, our behavior, and our thoughts. This does not mean we engage in morbid introspection. Rather, we simply take good, long looks at our lives, earnestly desire change, and ask the Holy Spirit to help us enact that change.

CONSIDER CHARLOTTE

C harlotte, thirty-eight, divorced for four years, has two children. She works as a secretary. Her salary plus child support from her ex-husband provides just enough money to make ends meet. She has nothing left over for the extras in life. She is outgoing, attractive, and usually good-humored. Right after her divorce, she accepted Christ, and now she attends church with Jack and Amy, the couple who led her to the Lord.

Lately Charlotte has been attending church only sporadically. She has gained weight—not much, but more than usual—and has given up her Saturdays out with the kids, which she used to look forward to, and instead has taken on extra typing jobs.

What tipped Charlotte's friends off to a problem was her decision to look for another church. She said her present church wasn't "meeting her needs."

When Amy asked why, Charlotte said, "I don't know I just need something more."

Amy questioned Charlotte further. "It's not your fault," Charlotte said. "But I don't know what else I can do."

Reluctantly, Charlotte wound up telling Amy about an incident that had happened four months before. She had been invited to Amy and Jack's house for a cookout. While Jack was barbecuing, Amy showed Charlotte their new sofa. As Charlotte looked at the sofa, waves of resentment rolled over her. Amy could afford a new sofa, yet she could not.

Outwardly she was casual, but during dinner her resentment mounted. Amy had Jack to help her with the kids. What did she have? A cold, lonely bed at night. Amy had a new sofa and a nice car. What did she have? An old car and furniture that was falling apart.

When Charlotte got home that night, she couldn't sleep. Bitterness, anger, and self-pity engulfed her. She told herself it was wrong to think such things. Amy and Jack were her best friends. They loved her. They were not trying to be prideful. Charlotte blocked her emotions.

A week later she ran into another friend, a woman with children in the local Christian school. That set Charlotte off on her second bout of jealousy. Why was this woman able to enroll *her* child in a Christian school when she couldn't? Didn't her children deserve Christian educations, too? How could God be so unfair?

As Charlotte began to look around the church, she became resentful toward other married women. Why did God allow them happiness but withhold it from her? Her ex-husband had married her when she was young and dumped her at thirty-four, an age at which men in general were scarce and Christian single men were all but nonexistent.

Restless and irritable, she quarrelled with friends over imagined slights and yelled at the kids. Then she panicked. She voraciously read all the passages of Scripture on covetousness and jealousy she could find. Guilt over her resentment compounded the resentment itself. Her attitude toward activities that had once been fun became "What's the use?" Her church attendance dropped off. That's when she decided to change churches.

Manipulating for Attention:
The Background for Her Thinking

Charlotte came from a middle-class home. Her parents provided for her adequately but showed her very little affection, not because they didn't love her, but because they believed that kids should "be serious and work hard for what they get." (A surprising number of parents simply do not *know how* to make their kids feel loved.) Nothing was done in Charlotte's family just because it was fun. A dress was bought because it was functional. The purpose of school was to prepare her for the future. Marriage was to give her a place in life.

Charlotte internalized her hurt over the lack of affection in her family: the times her father stiffened when she threw her arms around his neck, her mother's lack of comment on her accomplishments in school. Charlotte kept these things to herself. She looked and listened, and she learned. She learned to compensate for her hurt with an outgoing, bubbly personality. She learned that although she could not get affection from her family, she could get it by manipulating her friends for attention.

In high school, Charlotte was a cheerleader. She was in social clubs and was popular with both boys and girls. Her reward for her efforts was the warmth she received from those around her. She continued manipulating at the same rate in college, which brought her in touch with the man who was to be her husband. He was outgoing, spontaneous, and affectionate. He swept her off her feet. She married him. At first the marriage went well, but after several years, he began sharing his affection with women other than Charlotte.

When the marriage fell apart, Charlotte agonized. She remembered how her mother had criticized her cousin Elizabeth because of *her* divorce. Charlotte knew that her mother had considered Elizabeth a failure and had worried about whether or not she would be accepted back into her old circle of friends. Charlotte knew her family would not take her own divorce lightly.

After her divorce, Charlotte tried to console herself by remembering her ex-husband's faults, but that didn't ease her feeling of failure. She still felt that if somehow she had been prettier, sweeter, nicer, or smarter, the marriage would have worked. If she had worked harder, she would have had the love she needed.

Instead of discarding the kind of thinking that had produced her feeling of failure, Charlotte pulled herself together and relied on it again. She began going out. One of the places she went was church. The Christian community, like the secular community, provided an outlet for Charlotte's natural skill of manipulation. Only this time two things were different. Charlotte had accepted Christ as her Savior, and the warmth and love she found in the believers in Jesus Christ were different from anything she had ever known. Charlotte blossomed. For several years her friends in Christ and the genuine warmth of fellowship satisfied her craving for affection.

When covetousness and jealousy stirred in her heart, Charlotte was horrified. Why wasn't Christ "working"? What was the matter with her now? Because she wasn't attaining the goals she had been striving for all her life—to be loved, to be accepted, and to feel good—she felt she had no hope at all. She experienced deep despair. What if changing churches didn't help?

A Realistic Solution

Fortunately, Amy was a friend sensitive to God's will as well as to the emotional needs of others. By God's grace Charlotte's explanations of jealousy and anger did not threaten Amy's sense of worth and wholeness in the Lord. Instead of reacting defensively to her confession of anger, Amy tried to see beyond Charlotte's words to her true feelings.

Amy did not try to make Charlotte *feel* better. Rather than assuring her that everything would be okay, Amy wept with Charlotte. She agreed it *was* hard to live in a small apartment and work at a job for menial pay. It *did* hurt not to have a husband to love and help with the kids. But as compassionate as she was, Amy knew she was only human and could not heal the wounds causing Charlotte's pain. So she told Charlotte to cry out to God and tell him every emotion and anxiety she felt. She encouraged her to be specific, to reviw in her mind the exact incidents that had caused her jealousy. She told Charlotte to cry until she could cry no more.

As Christians, we must be realistic about the world we live in. Life isn't always fair. There was no use pretending that Charlotte's small apartment and aloneness were the same as Amy's home and husband. We must not bend reality to help God out of a seemingly tough spot. God can take care of himself.

The key for us is to learn to be still and allow God the space to reveal himself in whatever way he chooses. Amy knew this. She left Charlotte alone for a while to be with

God. Over the ensuing weeks Amy helped Charlotte comprehend the things she was seeing about herself.

The world comes crashing in on all of us sometimes. We can be grateful when it does. One Christian writer calls pain "God's megaphone." It's the instrument God often uses to get our attention and bring about the desired change in our lives. Reality came crashing in for Charlotte when she realized she was utterly helpless to do anything about her circumstances. The presence of a husband and the signs of prosperity in her friends' lives were painful reminders to Charlotte that she had not yet reached her goals.

Charlotte had to face the truth. She might not get all the things she thought she needed to be happy. She might not get the husband or move into the nice community her family thought was imporant. Her children might never attend the school she felt they needed. Although the warmth and affection she found in her church were genuine, they only intensified her pain and reminded her of the things she didn't have. Charlotte was alone and there was nothing that she, with her bubbly personality, could do about it.

Depression always comes from a blocked goal. As long as a woman feels there is any hope at all of reaching her goal, she'll keep on plugging, but once she perceives that she isn't going to reach that goal, she'll give up. The result is depression. Charlotte's problem was that she either denied the inequity she felt or thought there was no satisfaction possible without the good things she saw in her friends' lives. Her thinking ran: I can't have what I want, so I won't be happy with what I have. I won't accept the joys that are available if I can't have what I think should be mine in life.

Charlotte sincerely believed that since she could not manufacture sufficient love in her husband, her family, and her church, she had no hope of meeting her needs.

She had yet to accept her own deep sense of inadequacy and go broken to Christ. She had only gone to God in an attempt to manipulate him. All her well-meaning "Christian" activities—attending church, reading Scripture, praying fervently—had been performed with the wrong motive: to change how she felt.

Because Charlotte had never before acknowledged the wrongness of her motives, she had never felt completely helpless. Now, in her helplessness, she better understood the terrible inadequacy that humanity inherited from the Fall. Realizing that she had never appropriated the rest available in Christian redemption, she now longed for God's grace to move deeply within her.

Christian joy cannot be manufactured. It is an incomprehensible gift of God. The church does not exist to satisfy our neurotic desires. Each one of us has some problem which may never change. Our hope lies in Christ, in identifying ourselves with him.

Christ suffered in the Garden of Gethsemane as his friends fell asleep or deserted him. He died to the taunts of a jeering mob. But even in his suffering he never lost sight of heaven and never stopped trusting his Father. We can trust the Father too. We can become women of God, strong, bold, courageous, living life as it is.

It takes time to strip from our thinking the input of so many years. However, if our sole purpose is to become more like Christ, we will not be disappointed. As Charlotte began to trust God for whatever he chose to provide for her, she became free to love with the love of Jesus Christ. She found a love relationship that could not be broken.

Conclusion

Charlotte continued to change her thinking about the lousy circumstances in her life. She gradually learned to acknowledge her feeling of anger properly to God. And as a result of this, she developed more control over her actions.

Charlotte's changed thinking did not come about in an easy, one-two-three process, but gradually she saw the fallacy of thinking the solution to her personal problems was in changing her circumstances. Charlotte is closer now to being the woman God wants her to be than she has ever been before. At times she still gets angry about the inequity of her situation, but she expresses that anger to God and then reflects on the completeness of his love for her. She has peace and a greater measure of rational wholeness.

JUDI'S JOURNEY

*J*udi, twenty-six, unmarried, is intelligent, pretty, and well-liked by both men and women. Until recently, she held a good job with a prestigious banking firm in a large city. Ten months ago, however, after much prayer she decided to take a temporary leave of absence from her job and go back to school.

Judi had quit college in the middle of her senior year because she doubted the relevance of her studies to the real world. She wanted to find out for herself what was "important in life." After quitting school, she dabbled in existential philosophy and experimented with sex and drugs. Finding these did not satisfy her, she turned to the opposite extreme and began to pursue money and achievement through a high-powered career. She had been very successful in her career but still was not satisfied with her life.

Although Judi accepted Christ in high school, she dropped out of church when she dropped out of college. When the rise in her career brought her no peace, she decided to go back to church. The church where she now worships has just the right mixture of intellectual sophistication and orthodox Christian teaching to interest her. Since returning to church, she has grown so much that she has begun to seek God's will for her life. This is why she decided to go back to school. Although she knew returning to school would bring a temporary halt in her career, she felt it was God's will that she tie up the loose ends of her life before going on to anything else.

Shortly after returning to school, Judi began to experience feelings of severe tension, accompanied by back pain and occasional attacks of hyperventilation. In addition to this, Judi began missing her menstrual period. Her doctor told her there was no medical reason for the missed periods. He suggested she try to find the cause of her obvious emotional stress.

Judi had felt confident it was God's will that she return to school. Yet she was fearful that school might be what was causing her problems. During the ensuing days she maintained a cheerful and optimistic exterior, but she was thinking about a previous time in high school when she had reacted physically to emotional stress. When her father had been hospitalized for a nervous breakdown, she had developed a bleeding ulcer. Tension had caused her problem then, and apparently tension was the cause now. Judi, with her aggressive, take-hold personality, decided to make an appointment with the church counselor.

The Root of the Problem

The counselor began by asking Judi a few basic questions. When she asked, "Do you remember your mother's loving you? Do you remember being close to her?" Judi knew she was at a crossroad. She started to give a glib, cheerful response as she always had in the past, but the Holy Spirit whispered "Be real," and she started to cry. Actually, Judi had very few childhood memories of her mother. She said she could not remember being hugged or held. She said, "Truthfully, when it comes to my mother, my mind is blank." The counselor then asked Judi to give a family history.

Judi was a middle child. She had a sister three years older and a brother nine years younger. She was conceived just before the Korean War. Her father left for the army before Judi was born and did not return home until after she was four.

By the time her father returned, a pattern had already been established in Judi's life: her sister was clearly favored by her mother. Her preference was noticeable not only to Judi, but to friends of the family as well. It showed up in little things. Judi's sister was allowed to have long curly hair, but Judi had to keep her hair cut because "short hair was easier." Her mother listened in rapt attention to her sister's opinion or to her sister's playing the piano. But Judi's opinions and piano playing were all but ignored.

Judi remembered a time when the three of them were out shopping. Judi, age four, was allowed to wander off and wasn't missed until she finally had her mother paged at the Lost and Found. Even at a young age, Judi keenly felt the attitude of indifference.

When Judi's father returned home from the war, he must have noticed his wife's favoritism. He tried in his own way to make up to Judi for her mother's lack of attention. He took Judi under his wing, and she became her father's little girl. They took drives together. Sometimes she would go to work with him, and at lunch she would sit and talk with her dad and the other men. She would comb her father's hair and he would comb hers.

When she began school, she would come home and tell her dad about her day, and he, in turn, would tell her about his. They listened to each other.

When Judi got older, they took fishing trips together. They went to grandmother's house for the weekend— just the two of them. No one could doubt their affection for each other.

Then, when Judi was fourteen, her father suffered a nervous breakdown and was hospitalized for eighteen months. The family went bankrupt. With her father gone, Judi felt deserted, alone. Her mother and her sister, whom she had never been able to depend on anyway, fell apart. Contemptuous of her mother and sister because of their weakness, Judi thought to herself, "I'll never let anyone hurt me like that. They're acting immature. I'll act like an adult. I'll control my emotions my whole life long and no one will ever be able to hurt me."

Instead of giving in to her own feelings of loneliness and fear, Judi steeled herself against them. From that time on, she began to act. She acted as if she was happy when she was not. She acted as if she was sure of herself when she was afraid. She smiled when life got serious. She developed a strong, likeable personality and maintained control of her life.

As Judi began to change, the dynamics of her family also changed. With her father gone and the family in financial trouble, Judi assumed the role of head of the household. She kept her mother calm as she sat down with her to pay the family bills. Judi remembered her childhood surprise when she discovered electric lights were "not for free." Everything in life, she told herself, had a cost. A child of fourteen, who had been ignored by her mother, and had never been asked for an opinion before, was now making the major family decisions. When her father returned to the family, Judi continued the behavior that had served her so well—she kept her real emotions inside and continued to act.

In high school, like most teenagers, she wanted to be popular; but, for Judi, popularity was not just a desire, it was a necessity. She *had* to achieve and she did. She *had* to make good grades and she did. She *had* to be popular and she was.

For Judi, the normal desire to achieve and be well-liked became an obsession. It took precedence over her desire for affection and her desire for permanence. It kept her moving. She went out to parties and laughed a lot. She was popular with men, but she never stuck to any one man in particular—she was too "carefree" for that. It seemed nothing ever fazed Judi. Not popularity and good grades in high school; not sex, drugs, and alcohol after that; not success, money, and prestige later on. Nothing ruffled Judi's cool, cheerful exterior—until now.

Now Judi had discovered God, and he had made the difference in her life. Judi had found her match. Jesus Christ was not someone she could master and walk away from. God had taken hold of her heart. He wouldn't let go of her.

Right from the beginning, Judi knew she was taking a risk with God. But life itself had been so meaningless. She had to take a chance. Unconsciously, Judi reacted to God the same way she had reacted to everything else in her life. She was not sure she could trust him, so she decided to make the best of him.

She worked to be good for God just as she had worked to be good for Daddy. She devoured the works of C. S. Lewis and other Christian writers. She had a regular prayer time and Bible study each day. She attended church each Sunday. Judi worked hard to succeed. For example, she was characteristically serious about prayer.

Any old time was not good enough for prayer. She forced herself to rise at dawn and be cheerful while she prayed. While other people at her weekly prayer meeting shared their problems, Judi only praised God. As a practicing Christian, Judi felt more than ever she had to maintain appearances.

Although her motives were wrong, God honored Judi's efforts. She grew to the extent that she could no longer be contented with the direction of her life. It was then that she decided to take a new risk and go back to school. It was then that the tension began.

A Crack in the Wall

To the outside world and even to Judi herself, she seemed to be doing fine. But she wasn't. She had to break through the wall that surrounded her emotions in order to deal with her physical problems. Like many of us, Judi did not want to face her unacknowledged emotions that for years had so wrongly motivated her behavior.

Without the physical manifestation of her tension, Judi may never have taken that step. God works in supernatural ways. He is compassionate. He never leaves us to our own devices. Since Judi's desire to please God was genuine, even if it was wrongly motivated, God gave her courage and said to her, "Follow me." When Judi decided to go back to church, she took a risk. When she went back to school to be "simply a student," she took another risk. As a student Judi was just another face in the crowd, alone and unimportant. Since fourteen she had not allowed herself to be that vulnerable. Her props were gone. Her *act* became shaky and that's what produced her tension.

Opening herself up emotionally was a wrenching, painful, and exhausting experience for Judi, yet she felt

170

the Holy Spirit comforting and encouraging her to stop acting. Several months after her counseling sessions, Judi's menstrual periods resumed their normal pattern.

Once she recognized the unacknowledged emotions that had motivated her behavior for so long, she was anxious to change. First she concentrated on freeing her emotions and correcting her thinking; but that was only the first step in experiencing personal worth. She needed to learn to take more risks.

Her biggest risk was electing not to take a part-time job while attending school. She did this to allow herself more time for intimate fellowship with other believers, a new thing for Judi. She had always been afraid of deep friendships in the past. Also, not working allowed her bank account to dwindle, which was also new to Judi. She reasoned that if she didn't have extra money as a cushion, she would genuinely learn to trust God. She decided this was one time she wasn't going to play it safe.

Judi still has a tendency to block emotions she doesn't want to deal with, but now her cheerfulness is real. Judi, like all of us, knows our wholeness is never complete until we reach heaven. However, the emotional freedom she feels today brings her deep and real joy.

Conclusion

Several months after her counseling, Judi went home for Christmas. She had prayed for an opportunity to talk openly and intimately with her mother. God was quick in opening a door. Three days after she arrived, Judi's mom invited her to take a walk with her in the woods behind their house. After walking for a while in silence, Judi asked casually, "Mom, was there anything particularly difficult going on in the family when I was a child?"

171

Her mother looked past Judi into the woods and didn't answer for a moment. Then she said, "Judi, your father and I were extremely happy right before you were conceived. In fact, it was because we were so happy together that we decided we wanted you. You were the only one of our children who was ever truly planned.

"Then, before you were born, your father went into one of his mental depressions and deserted me and your sister who was only three years old. I barely scraped by. I was desperate. I took a warrant out for your father's arrest because I needed child support. In order to leave town he joined the army and didn't come back for more than four years."

When her mother finished talking, Judi asked softly, "Mom, did I always look just like my dad?"

Her mother said, "Judi, you were always the spitting image of your father."

Judi understood. They touched and hugged and then walked back to the house in silence.

172

MEET MICHEL

CHAPTER 14

Michel, twenty-eight, never married, is an artist. In many ways her life resembles the stereotype of a "typical artist." She is spacy and given to mood swings. Involved first in one project, then another, she lives her life on the edge of constant crisis.

Michel is never alone in her various crises, however. She always has friends to help her through them. Michel considers her friends her best asset, like having gold in reserve. She says she doesn't see how she could get along without them.

Although Michel is an artist, her main source of income is derived from a small art gallery she owns and operates. In six years of business she has built up an excellent clientele and enjoys her work.

A Christian since she was seventeen, Michel is also very active in her church. She feels about Christ the same way she does about her friends—she doesn't know how she could get along without him.

On the whole, Michel likes her life. She feels it's exciting and interesting. One thing Michel doesn't like, however, is her "marshmallow personality." She knows she's undisciplined and irresponsible, that she sometimes makes three appointments in one evening, not because she's forgotten about them, but because she genuinely wants to say yes to everyone.

She works five to six days nonstop and then falls in a heap for three days to recuperate. Because she is a binge eater, first overeating and then starving herself, her weight fluctuates fifteen pounds up and down. She lets her bills pile up unopened because she doesn't want to face what's inside, and she accepts more commissions than she can handle because she doesn't want to "turn anyone down."

Michel knows that her behavior is undisciplined and therefore sinful. She considers herself spineless and laments her lack of character. Although she has prayed many times for God to help her with her lack of self-discipline, nothing much has happened yet.

One afternoon Michel arrived in the office of a professional counselor. Tearfully she told the counselor she was in the midst of the worst financial year of her life. She acknowledged that her undisciplined lifestyle had finally caught up with her and that she was falling apart. The counselor asked her to be more specific about what had prompted her anxiety. She replied that in good times her lack of self-discipline didn't matter much, but with the current state of the economy her life was a disaster. She said that what had prompted her to make this visit was the feeling of hysteria she had all the time.

Looking at Her Childhood

Michel was an only child. Her mother had been the less favorite of two daughters and had grown up during the depression. Her father was the good-looking son of a moderately wealthy woman. Michel's mother had spent her childhood struggling to survive, while her father had left home at eighteen to drink and tour the world.

Michel's childhood memories are that her father never stopped drinking and her mother never stopped trying to survive.

When the counselor suggested Michel tell him more about her relationship with her mother, she described her mother as the one who held the family together, who worked to save while her father worked to drink. Michel said her place in the family was to perform—not in the traditional sense of washing dishes, making beds, going to school, and making good grades. Oddly enough, she was never expected to do these things. Instead Michel was expected to be popular, look pretty, have nice clothes, and lead an "interesting and exciting" life. She was expected to do what her mother had never had the opportunity to do in her childhood. Michel did not disappoint her mother—she performed with gusto. She succeeded in fulfilling her mother's dreams.

What she remembered most was how her mother had always done her work for her. She did the dishes while Michel did her nails. She made Michel a dress while Michel slept. If Michel did set the table, her mother straightened it. Before she died, her mother gave Michel money to open an art gallery. Michel remembered her mother saying anxiously many times, "Honey, I don't want you ever to be unhappy."

Aside from her mother's influence, she felt that the next most telling thing about her was her involvement with men, not boyfriends necessarily, but men in general. She attributed the importance of men in her life to the fact that they tended to "look out for her." Men could be relied upon to help her through the various states of panic or confusion she tended to make of her life.

175

The counselor, who was a Christian, asked Michel about her faith. She told him that was why she had come. She couldn't understand why, when she asked God to help her be more self-disciplined, he had not done so. She stated emphatically, "I don't want to be a marshmallow anymore, and I don't believe it's God's will that I be one either." She then broke down and cried. She said her biggest frustration was that her friends didn't take her seriously. They always attributed her problems to being "artistic." Or they would say, "Oh, everyone does that!"

In frustration she told the counselor, "They don't consider what I'm struggling with very important. Please believe me. I know that being a marshmallow is not God's will for me. It gets me into so much trouble."

A Long Road

It was five years before Michel was able to experience her true worth in Christ and make any significant change in her ability to act volitionally. Her situation illustrates the point that behavior change is a *process*. Generally speaking, plateaus build one upon another. In this case, there were three pivotal points that prompted change. The first two had to do with assertiveness. The last involved risk taking.

Michel's mother was the major influence in her life. Her loving but misguided effort to protect her daughter from the unhappiness she herself had felt as a child had unwittingly kept Michel from developing a healthy inner strength. When her mother reset the table after Michel, she indicated to Michel that she had not done it right, but she did not show her the right way to do it. When she stayed up all night to make Michel a dress, she emphasized the importance of looking pretty and pleasing others but did not teach Michel how to sew. When her mother did the dishes while Michel did her nails, Michel learned that everyday responsibilities could be avoided. She did not learn the value of responsible behavior.

Michel loved her mother very much, so as she watched her anxious mother doing her work for her, she discerned a message: Your mother is so worried about you there must be something to worry about. Your mother is so afraid you'll do things wrong, you must not be able to do them right.

No one, not even a six year old, wants to experience the pain of failure. As a result Michel began to avoid situations in which she might fail. She refused to do anything her mother could do well. She stopped doing housework, homework, or simple chores of any kind. Rather, Michel excelled in areas outside her mother's experience. She was creative and socially successful. She had lots of friends and manipulated them to do her work for her, the way she had manipulated her mom. While Michel managed to have the interesting and exciting life her mother felt was important, Michel missed the joy of diligent effort. She missed the thrill of hard work well done. Because of her mother's protection, Michel experienced no sense of personal worth whatsoever. She felt like a zero inside.

Michel was not being falsely spiritual when she said God and her friends were the most important things in her life. No one, not even Michel, would have been able to manipulate people the way she had were it not for the fact that she honestly believed she could not function without her friends' help. Michel was not being deceptive; she really *believed* she was helpless.

This brings about the other side of this coin. Michel attracted both men and women who *wanted* to help her, who needed to be needed. This is one of the reasons she could never say no to others. She genuinely wanted to show her appreciation for all they did for her. This is also why no one really took her seriously. For the most part, they liked the way she was. Her helplessness met their needs as well.

Michel's wrong thinking also affected her relationship with Christ. This is how she could emphatically state that she didn't want to be a marshmallow any longer. "When is *God* going to change me!" she wanted to know. Her thinking had extended to her theology. Her lack of success apart from others caused her to believe she really was helpless, and because of her helplessness, "Christ *had* to help her." She was not a sinner in need of grace. She was a marshmallow in need of support. She was not a strong woman humbled by her sinful nature. She was a woman who saw herself as a nothing. God was not her strength; God was her crutch.

The counselor worked first on Michel's inability to say no, on making decisions and standing strong once decisions were made. They worked for several months, and some progress was made. Then, one day Michel came into the office late and upset. She said she had run out of gas again, as usual.

To his horror, the counselor discovered that running out of gas was a monthly event for Michel. He looked her straight in the eye and said, "Michel, why would you *choose* such inconvenient behavior?" Michel had never thought of crises as being a matter of choice before.

At the end of that session, the counselor had correctly analyzed that Michel, in addition to feeling like a zero, unknowingly, felt it was *necessary* to be weak. She had observed the interaction between her mother and father. She had seen her mother struggle to support her father, and Michel thought, "I won't let this happen to me. Because I'm a zero and not able to take care of anyone else, I'll act helpless. That way, I won't attract anyone I have to support."

As a result of this thinking, Michel attracted both men and women to support her. She skillfully held her life together by shirking responsibility and then allowing others to rescue her. This is what accounted for so much confusion and chaos in her life.

Again the counselor looked Michel in the eye and said, "Michel, you are not a weak woman. You are a strong woman. Your behavior is false and dangerous. You need to know, since you are single, that your actions may be attracting the type of man that cannot give you the emotional strength you need. It is in your own best interest to be the strong woman you are."

From that day Michel's life changed. She increased the fees on her paintings by four hundred percent. She said no to conflicting appointments. She became assertive. Though her life was less hectic, her problems were far from over. Her bills still piled up on her desk, her house was either immaculately clean or a mess. She gained or lost weight at an unhealthy rate. Michel had learned to say no to others, but she had not learned to say yes to herself. She had not learned that she herself was a person of worth—worthy of paid bills and an orderly house.

Moving Along

One day while driving to pick up some paintings in another state, Michel was on the lookout for a rest stop. She saw a roadside gift shop and stopped to use the rest room. When she came out, she felt that she *had* to buy something. After all, she had used their facilities. She felt that she had to repay them in some way. She looked at the tacky shell ashtrays, the fattening candies, the toys for two years olds, and then in her usual pattern of thinking, decided, "I just can't use their facilities and not buy something."

As Michel looked around, she heard a voice within. "Michel, it's okay to have needs and not always meet other people's expectations." She hesitated. She looked at the woman behind the counter. The woman smiled. Michel smiled back and said, "Thank you so much."

"That's okay. Have a nice trip."

Michel got into the car. Her heart soared. She was free! For the first time she had not been obligated by other people's expectations. She knew she was responsible to God for her actions, but she no longer had to live for the approval of others.

Assertiveness for Michel was a learned behavior. It was not a deep, ingrained belief in her worth in Jesus Christ. She became a strong woman because she was afraid of attracting a weak man. She traded manipulative ploys for assertive technique. When she became assertive, she was not being a marshmallow anymore.

It's important to note that all behavior has purpose. Until a woman can perceive God's purposes, until she can comprehend her worth and true value in Christ, much of her behavior is likely to be superimposed. Trading one wrongly motivated behavior for another is not the solution.

The counselor realized this and continued to work with Michel. But not until Michel herself realized she didn't have to buy something she didn't want to please someone she didn't know for doing something that wasn't rude, did she know she was on her way to wholeness.

Two years had passed from the time Michel first went to see the counselor. Her manipulative behavior had changed and she was experiencing and acting on her worth in Christ, but she wanted more than that. She wanted to spend her life telling others about Christ. She wanted to use her craft and her artwork to develop a ministry with women—to tell them that Christ *does* change lives.

Plenty of support for her plan came from others. Her only problem was that in order to have enough time to develop a ministry, Michel had to be organized and highly efficient. This was something she had never been before! She prayed. She definitely felt it was God's will for her to move in that direction. She analyzed her life and realized the only way she could carry out her desire was to decrease her overhead and increase her productivity.

After more prayer and planning, she let her manager and her assistant go, she moved her painting studio into the back of the gallery, and she worked and waited on the customers herself. She closed her shop two days a week and began to develop her ministry.

Three months after making this drastic move, Michel became depressed. Her back ached, her head ached, and she was listless and unmotivated. Although she had enough time to do her work, she allowed it to pile up to the point of being overpowering.

Michel went back to the counselor for help. He said to her, "Michel, you're procrastinating because you want this so desperately and are afraid of failure. Although you experience your worth in Christ, and have made much progress over the years, you're still unwilling to test your capacities to the fullest. You're afraid of pushing yourself to the limit. You're afraid that if you test your abilities and fail, it will prove again what you have believed all your life—that you're a failure, a nothing, a zero. Risk is involved in anything we do, Michel. You may fail, but if you don't try, you'll never know for sure. So why not try?"

The counselor then said something to Michel that no one had ever said to her before—not her mother, not her friends, not her co-workers. He said, "Michel, do it yourself!"

She did.

Conclusion

I am Michel. Although many details in the story have been changed, the problems were mine. Michel's struggle for volitional wholeness was mine. I wrote this book while running my business, putting my son through college, and helping with the affairs of my elderly father.

God's strength is made perfect in weakness. To him be the glory!

O HAPPY ONES AND HOLY!

CHAPTER 15

O, happy ones and holy!
Lord give us grace that we,
Like them the meek and lowly,
On high may dwell with Thee.

—*The Church's One Foundation*

Four years have passed since I wrote the stories of Charlotte, Judi, and Michel. A lot has happened since that time.

Charlotte still has her pleasing, bubbling personality and others are still drawn to her, but now they're attracted by her deep inner faith. Her apartment is clean and tidy with plants all around. A beautiful hand-crocheted shawl covers her old sofa.

But the best and most surprising change for Charlotte is the change in her relationship with her two children. She is willing to "let them go." Before her crisis with anger, she unknowingly demanded love from her children just as she demanded love from everyone else. Now she says, "I love my kids for who they are. I love them the way I longed to be loved all my life."

Predictably, Judi graduated from college with honors. She returned to her old job and is already in line for upper-echelon management. In touch with her emotions, she's beginning to feel deeply that she's not married. "Before," she said, "I didn't want a husband because I didn't want the pain of being involved in a real relationship. Now, I think I'm ready." For the last six months Judi has been dating a co-worker. Ambitious himself, he's attracted to Judi because of her drive. But he's even more attracted because of her faith.

The last time I spoke to Judi she said, "You know, I think one of the reasons I never married was that I didn't believe I could ever leave Daddy. With Paul, I'm willing to take that risk."

Michel is excited by her ministry to other single women. She laughs and says, "See God's faithfulness even to those of us who don't *always* have it all together!" She's glad to be able to tell others of God's love and his grace.

Writing this book over a several-year period has given me an opportunity to see God's handiwork in the intricate patterns of women's lives. Of those I initially interviewed, two have married. Another has ended a five-year relationship with a man she thought she couldn't live without. A secretary has started a small business in her off hours. Two women have organized ministries on their own. A married woman who was thinking of a divorce is now teaching a course on marriage and the family. Another woman has quit her job and is enrolling in law school. A woman who didn't think she could save a penny has opened an IRA. The list could go on.

What do I see as the central theme in all this? That it's good to tell women to stand strong and gut it out. We don't have to live with a superficial Christianity, with "feel good" religion which offers a Band-Aid for a gushing wound. For Christianity to work, really work, there must come a time when we face our pain and are healed by the love of God.

Because I've seen what God can do not only in my life but in the lives of others, let me encourage you. Build a network of friends among your Christian brothers and sisters. Don't use them or hide in fear. Open your heart. Be kind. Love your friends. If, at times, loneliness overwhelms you and you ache for a godly man to love you and one doesn't, turn to God. Experience sweet communion with the Father.

At work, think about the unique way God created you and how God can use you in your job. Think through the ethical issues of your work. Use your gifts. Look for ways you can serve your boss and your co-workers. Bring order into your work and your life. When you come home tired, know that you've been doing your Father's business. He's proud of you.

Being women of courage doesn't necessarily mean we'll go down in the annals of church history. Maybe we'll simply struggle with the everyday problems of life. Done God's way, that's extremely heroic.

The Search

I believe now more than ever Christian single women are God's untapped resource. Today in America, 42 percent of women over the age of forty are single. As the baby-boom generation approaches that age, the percentage will increase.

Single women, young and old, are looking for meaning and purpose in life. We live with the effects of the sexual revolution, the feminist movement, a drug culture, threats of war, and economic uncertainty. It's exhausting.

God's love is a soft place.

It's in the midst of the impossible, the improbable, the stuff we never thought we could live through that opportunity comes. Like the woman who met Jesus at the well, having tasted of the living water and being refreshed, we go to our neighbors and say, "Come, see a Man who told me all things that I ever did" (John 4:29).

The Reward

Let's not only eschew superficial Christianity and face the pain of life, let's go one step further. Let's pursue holiness.

Holiness is a refining fire. It's what makes our faith pure gold. If we're ever to go out into the world, we have to go with something that comes from within, that comes from God himself—holiness.

Yet most of us, me included, are afraid of holiness. We're afraid of the idea, even the word. R. C. Sproul identifies this response as the "trauma of holiness," in his book *The Holiness of God*. It's a sinful person's discomfort with the idea of perfect purity. We miss the challenge, "Be holy, for I am holy" (1 Pet. 1:16) because we're intimidated by the very word God has called us to be. And we miss the opportunity to be truly happy.

Holiness exposes the attitude of the heart as nothing else can. It forces us to see beyond the mild agitation of surface sins to the baseness of our own souls. The reality of sin evokes a sense of our helplessness apart from Jesus Christ. And this, believe it or not, brings us an unexpected reward—happiness. The reverential fear of God that comes in the light of his holiness allows us to see God's tender mercy.

"There is a satisfaction that comes with righteous living that can be obtained no other way," according to Steve Brown. Any time we fail to link the idea of satisfaction and joy to the godly life, we run the risk of not longing for the rewards of righteous living. We end up feeling guilty about wanting to be happy and fearing to be holy.

Holiness inspires one last thought. This is the idea of separation. Holiness means to be set apart for God's use. I believe this concept causes us more hesitation than our reverential fear of him. We're afraid to risk standing alone.

Yet how good it is to think about what our lives can be like, how we can be strong, have dominion over our world, become totally abandoned in the face of God's love. How exciting to imagine ourselves grandly, nobly set apart, women dedicated to God's use.

Jesus said we would remember always a woman who had such courage and love.

> And being in Bethany at the house of Simon the leper, as He sat at the table, a woman came having an alabaster flask of very costly oil of spikenard. And she broke the flask and poured it on his head.

> But there were some who were indignant among themselves, and said, "Why was this fragrant oil wasted? For it might have been sold for more than three hundred denarii and given to the poor." And they criticized her sharply.

But Jesus said, "Let her alone. Why do you trouble her? She has done a good work for Me. For you have the poor with you always, and whenever you wish you may do them good; but Me you do not have always. She has done what she could. She has come beforehand to anoint My body for burial. Assuredly, I say to you, wherever this gospel is preached throughout the whole world, what this woman has done will also be told as a memorial to her." (Mark 14:3–9)

Many people surrounded Jesus, yet this woman seemed to be the only one who comprehended what was happening to him. Christ was going to die.

What a rare quality clear-sightedness is.

This woman grasped the importance of the moment. She didn't try to explain away her fears. She faced the fact that her Lord was in danger, and after thinking about what that meant, she felt deeply the emotion of the situation.

But no matter how good clear-sightedness is, if that were all we learned from this woman, hers would be a desperate and depressing story. But it's not, because you see, she not only faced Christ's impending death and felt fully what that would mean to her, she also *did* something about the situation. She possessed perfume worth a year's wages and she chose to spend it all in one grand moment anointing the Lord's body.

This woman did all she could with what she had. We can do that, too. What we have isn't important; what's important is we give it all to Christ.

I love this woman because she was so feminine. She possessed perfume in a beautiful alabaster jar. How womanly. Jesus didn't accuse her of frivolity. He didn't ask, "Why aren't you more serious?" He simply allowed her to give her gift to him and then said to the others, "Leave her alone. She will be remembered always."

What do you have right now to offer Christ?

Perhaps you don't think you're spiritual enough to be truly dedicated to Christ. Or maybe you don't believe that you're capable of any great act of faith. You don't need to be anyone special to serve the Lord. You simply need to know the One you love.

The woman with the alabaster jar will be remembered always because she understood. If no one else was willing to show love for Christ, she was. Even if her gifts were different and unacceptable to others, they were hers and she was willing to give.

What do you suppose could produce a determination that strong? The love of the One she loved. The woman was responding to what she had already experienced in the love of God. It was his love that helped her go beyond deep personal pain and give her all to him.

Do you know that we can do that, too? We can be totally abandoned and totally unafraid to give our all to Christ. We can be the godly women he has called us to be. No matter what the price, wholeness is worth it.

Beloved sisters, we are women with a future. We can give our all to Christ gladly, lay down our lives every day, day after day, make good choices, and gain the deep and penetrating joy that comes from such total commitment.

We can know what it is to be truly happy.

This is not the end of a book. It's a beginning. With clear minds we can begin to comprehend the benefits of virtue and the reward of a godly life. By his grace we can move beyond singleness to become women of God.

Chapter 5

1. C.S. Lewis, *Mere Christianity* (New York: Macmillan, 1952), p. 109.
2. "Marriage and Divorce Today," *The Professional Newsletter,* June 8, 1980.

Chapter 6

1. Janis Handler, "Corporate Trust on the Feminine Mystique," *Wall Street Journal,* March 25, 1985, Managers Journal Column.
2. "More and More She's the Boss," *Time,* December 2, 1985.

Chapter 7

1. Fred Smith, *You and Your Network* (Waco, Texas: Word Books, 1984), p. 46.

Chapter 10

1. Nancy A. Hardesty, *Great Women of Faith* (Grand Rapids: Michigan: Baker Book House, 1980), pp. 15-19.
2. Ibid.
3. Ibid., pp. 71-75.
4. Ibid., pp. 103-107.

Chapter 11

1. Lawrence J. Crabb, Jr., and Dan B. Allender, *Encouragement: The Key to Caring* (Grand Rapids, Michigan: Zondervan, 1980), pp. 28-29.
2. Ibid.
3. Ibid.
4. Lawrence J. Crabb, Jr., *Institute of Biblical Counseling Training Manual* (1978), p. 36.
5. Ibid., p. 11.
6. Ibid., p. 36-37.